Sashiko

Sashiko

Easy & Elegant Japanese Designs for Decorative Machine Embroidery

MARY S. PARKER

LARK BOOKS

Asheville, North Carolina

To my mother,

Lydia Mary

Crissey Saltsman Pickett,

and to the memory

of my father,

Wilbur Yost Saltsman

Editor: Dawn Cusick

Art Director: Dana Irwin

Photographer: Sandra Stambaugh

Illustrators: Hannes Charen (pattern dictionary), Orrin Lundgren

Production Assistants: Hannes Charen, M.E. Kirby

Editorial Assistants: Heather S. Smith, Catharine Sutherland

Japanese Language Consultant: Jun Kamata

Library of Congress Cataloging-in-Publication Data

Available

10 9 8 7 6 5 4 3 2 1

First Edition

Published by Lark Books
50 College St.
Asheville, NC 28801, US

© 1999, Lark Books

For information about distribution in the U.S., Canada, the U.K.,
    Europe, and Asia, call Lark books at 828-253-0467.

Distributed in Australia by Capricorn Link (Australia) Pty Ltd.,
    P.O. Box 6651, Baulkham Hills Business Centre, NSW 2153,
Australia

Distributed in New Zealand by Southern Publishers Group, 22
    Burleigh St., Grafton, Auckland, NZ

Printed in China by Donnelley Bright Sun Printing Company, Ltd.

ISBN 1-57990-132-8

CONTENTS

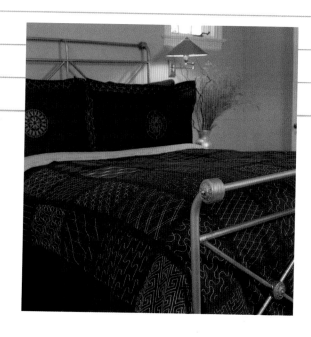

Introduction

The designs used in sashiko also appear in other media such as printed textiles and pottery. The pottery above, by Ransmeier Studios, shows the katabami and yabane patterns.

In her younger years, my mother was an artist and teacher. During his working career, my father was a time and motion engineer and a research and development shop supervisor. As one might expect, my parents saw the world from quite different perspectives and often did not get along with each other very well. However, by some stroke of good fortune, I seem to have inherited an aptitude for both their sets of skills along with a knack for integrating them.

I decided long ago that my particular gift was discovering how to make beautiful things—very efficiently.

It has been nearly a decade since I first encountered sashiko in an evening lecture/demo class taught by a wonderful woman named Johanna Verkammen. I loved the traditional sashiko designs immediately, but I was distressed by the tedious traditional method of marking the cloth in order to be able to sew those designs.

I have a passion for making the most of my sewing time because I have relatively little of it. I also pursue another full-time career in addition to my designing and teaching. My other career satisfies many aspects of my nature, but I have found

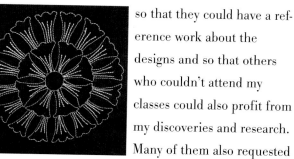

that only by designing, teaching, and sewing can I seem to satisfy the craving in my soul to be creative. Over the last decade, I have been on a quest to discover the best methods of marking and sewing sashiko, methods that produce the most beautiful results with the least amount of error and effort.

I have taught my method of "deciphering" sashiko patterns to find continuous stitching lines to hundreds of students over the past several years. In addition to providing hands-on experience with color coding and sewing the designs, I also always tell my students the history and cultural significance of the sashiko patterns that they will sew. Their enthusiastic reactions to this background information have reinforced my belief that most of us enjoy sewing a design even more when we can experience it on many different levels—as a symbol and part of a cultural tradition, as well as a thing of beauty and proportion.

Over the years, many of my students have urged me to write a book: both

so that they could have a reference work about the designs and so that others who couldn't attend my classes could also profit from my discoveries and research. Many of them also requested me to keep developing original designs made specifically for continuous sewing.

This book is the outgrowth of all those requests. If the designs and projects contained in it provide fashion sewers, quilters, and fabric lovers with some of the same enjoyment that I have gotten from researching, writing, and sewing for the book, I shall be very pleased. I am most grateful to the staff at Lark Books for having given me this wonderful opportunity and for having worked so hard to turn my dream for a book into a most beautiful reality.

SASHIKO: A Window to Japan's Cultural History

Woodblock print of the Province of Kai by Katsushika Hokusai (1760-1849)

Sashiko arose in the humblest of circumstances. Japanese peasants originally developed a running-stitch technique that they called "little stabs" to patch torn and worn clothing. Until the 18th century, cloth and thread were especially scarce and valuable. (An entirely new garment was seldom to be had and was worn only on special occasions.)

Areas of a garment that received the most wear were patched most frequently. These varied with the primary occupation of the peasant. A fisherman's clothing was likely to have layers of patches in the knee/shin area of the trousers and on the underside of the arms because the fabric in these areas abraded as the fisherman knelt in the boat and pulled in the net. A farmer's clothing was likely to have layers of patches in the shoulder, upper back, and neck area because heavy items were carried around the farm by hanging two buckets off either end of a pole that was balanced across the farmer's upper back and shoulders, causing the fabric to wear in some areas from the friction from the slight swing of the pole as the farmer walked. The sole of the two-toed socks that both farmers and fisherman wore under their sandals was also likely to be patched many more times than the upper areas of the sock.

Patching was originally done with thread made from the same fiber as the garment. Because the thread did not contrast with the garment fabric, designs were chosen primarily for their utility. Over the centuries, however, undyed (white) cotton thread gradually became available, and it contrasted strikingly with the indigo-dyed fabric used for garments. Once the stitching used to patch a garment became readily visible, more elaborate designs began to develop. Peasants cherished even small bits of cotton thread for their value in sashiko mending. Because the cotton thread used was already in small pieces, designs that required the stitching to be stopped and tied were not a disadvantage.

The most common fabric available to the Japanese peasants was made from hemp or other bast-rooted plants. These fabrics were not especially good insulators, so peasants prepared for cold weather by donning multiple layers of clothing. When cotton thread became more readily available and did not have to be reserved for patching garments, layers of clothing were permanently quilted together for winter wear. This quilting created air pockets that vastly improved insulating capacity. Old or outgrown clothing thus came to be recycled into everyday patchwork outerwear garments that were both adorned with and held together by sashiko stitching.

In the 18th and 19th centuries, sashiko stitching began to be practiced as much for its decorative value as for its original utilitarian purpose. As the stitching technique filtered upward from the peasants into the merchant classes of society, it lost its association with mending and became an artistic medium.

For example, during the Edo or Tokugawa period (1603 through 1868) that ended centuries of civil war, displaced soldiers turned to firefighting as an occupation. There was certainly need for this service in

newly urbanized Japan. Fires were so common that they were called the flowers of Edo. Sashiko was used to quilt layers of whole-cloth coats together as protective firefighting gear. These quilted coats were drenched with water before the firefighter approached the burning structure. The more elaborately embellished side of the garment was worn to the inside to protect it during the actual firefighting. The coat was turned to show its best side during the frequent parades to honor the firefighters. The sashiko designs that adorn these coats are often quite fanciful and playful.

Today in Japan, sashiko is a major national hobby. The Japanese are rightfully proud of their distinctive style of quilting, wherein patterns are made with contrasting thread on whole cloth. However, many modern Japanese quilters also use typical sashiko designs in Western style piecework quilts. Sashiko designs cover a particularly broad spectrum because the stitching technique profited from so many different influences over the past two millennia.

Some sashiko designs—probably the very oldest—are also found in many other cultures. These patterns are geometrical and are formed by counting warp and weft threads in the base fabric to determine where the individual sashiko stitches should be placed. Developing independently in many different locations, these designs appear to have been embedded in the human consciousness. The *hishi-igeta* or *tasuki* pattern (design 1:10) and the *uroko* patterns (designs 1:14 through 1:16) are both examples of very ancient straight-line motifs that have been found on prehistoric Japanese ceramics. These designs therefore belong to the period of Japanese prehistory called the Jomon period (8000 B.C. to 300 B.C.)

A large number of sashiko patterns were derived from Chinese designs. Japan is thought to have made first contact with China during the Yayoi period (300 B.C. to A. D. 300). Japanese culture continued to be closely modeled after the Chinese until well into the Heian Period (A. D. 794 to 1185). However, many of these "Chinese" patterns were not indigenous to China, but had traveled there on the "Silk Road." The designs had actually originated in India, Persia, or even Greece.

Artifacts from the Tumulus period (A. D. 300 to 552) demonstrate this cross-cultural effect clearly. The *seigaiha* pattern of overlapping waves (design 7:8) that decorates the cloth-

The Golden Temple, Kyoto, Japan

ing of Haniwa clay figures from the Tumulus period was used in ancient Persia long before it was used in China.

Buddhism had been imported to Japan from Korea at the beginning of the Asuka period (A.D. 552 to 710). Some sashiko designs such as *shippo* (design 2:3) and *manji* (design 5:14) were derived directly from Buddhist symbols . Some other sashiko patterns became associated with Buddhism simply because they arrived in Japan about the same time. In this later category are designs that imitated woven or embroidered designs on textiles, most of which were imported from China. The very name of the *sayagata* patterns (designs 3:12 and 3:14) indicates its

origin as an imitation of "silk weave." However, the pattern can be found on at least one building in Greece whose construction considerably predates the use of the design in brocades.

The Asuka period is also notable for having produced the oldest surviving piece of sashiko-stitched clothing. It is a robe that had been worn by a Buddhist priest and was reportedly owned by the Emperor Shomu, before his widow donated it to a temple in A. D. 756. It is now housed in the Shosoin Repository.

Chinese influence peaked during the Nara (A. D. 710 to 794) and Heian (A.D. 794 to 1185) periods. Designs imported from China were used almost exclusively. Among them were *kikko* (tortoiseshell) of designs 5:5

and 7:7, *karabana* (Chinese flower) of design 4:12), *inazuma* (lightning) of designs 3:11 and 3:23, and *kiku* (chrysanthemum) of design 6:7. Designs featuring *fuji* (wisteria) such as design 6:5 were also popular because the ruling Fujiwara family's name literally translated as field of wisteria. Other sashiko designs were taken directly from the Chinese writing system of ideographs known in Japan as *kanji*. Examples of these are *juji* (the ten of design 3:4) and *tsumeta* (the rice field of design 7:4).

In the midtenth century, Lady Murasaki Shikibu wrote the world's first novel, *The Tale of the Genji*. Stories from it are still performed in Noh theater plays in Japan. The motifs on the costumes used in these productions are generally those that were popular during the Heian period. However, during the late Heian period, boredom with Chinese designs began to set in. As a reflection of a growing national sensibility, *sakura*, or the "cherry blossom," came to be designated the national flower of Japan. Other indigenous Japanese plants began to become popular as design motifs. New abstract designs, such as *tatewaku* (rising steam) and *chidori* (plovers), also gained in popularity. Commoners began to use lateral stripes to decorate their clothing.

Traditional Geisha costume

The next few centuries saw Japan engaged in almost continuous civil war. During the Kamakura period (1185 to 1336) family crests or *mon*, which had been used only incidentally during the previous Heian period, were institutionalized and embroidered on outer layers of clothing as a way of identifying the allegiance of individual combatants. Armies assembled under flags imprinted with the crest of their Shogun. The warrior class often created their crests by inserting a broad-sword blade into a botanical design that had been created in the earlier period. Many of the *mon* (literally translated

as thread markings) eventually provided inspiration for sashiko patterns. It was during the Kamakura period that *kiku* (chrysanthemum) became the crest of the imperial family.

The Muromachi (1336 to 1568) and Azuchi-Momoyama (1568 to 1600) periods experienced great political instability. Families splintered and reformed as the fortunes of war shifted. Family crests were continuously modified to reflect changed martial and marital alliances. A large number of variants on the original, basic crest designs thus emerged. Crests that originally had a circular shape were morphed into diamonds and vice-versa.

During the Muromachi and Azuchi-Momoyama periods, the Noh theater came into prominence. Japan's capital had been moved to Kyoto, which was the center of the Japanese silk textile industry. Consequently, Noh productions in the capital had access to sumptuous silk fabric for their costumes. The Noh theater's convention of using a single, repeated pattern, such as *kikko*, *uroko*, or *matsukawa bishi* over the whole garment gradually influenced the design of other Japanese textiles. Stripes were also commonly used.

In contrast to the immediately preceding periods, the Tokugawa, or Edo, period (1600 to 1868) was one of sustained peace and self-imposed isolationism. In this era, sashiko reached its zenith. With the expansion of the cotton industry within Japan, cotton thread, the primary material necessary for sashiko, became more readily available than ever. During the Edo period, inspiration for design also literally surrounded the common folk, and popular culture influenced Japanese society in a completely unprecedented way. The semiannual procession of courtiers to and from the imperial city of Edo (Tokyo) gave even rural-dwelling commoners an opportunity to gain design inspiration from the finery of the noble classes. In cities, the various classes of Japanese society came into contact with each other as never before. For example, the firefighting companies mentioned earlier included both members of the warrior class and commoners.

During this period of Japan's isolation from the outside world, emphasis was placed on creating purely Japanese designs. Books of motifs were published to provide models for use as ceramic, woodcarving, and textile patterns. We know the name of

only one of the authors, Katsushika Hokusai (1760 to 1849), but the basic form of many modern-day sashiko designs can be found in his works. Many of these designs were taken from items used in everyday life including *ishiguruma* (stone cart wheel), *fundo* (counterweights), *kagome* (woven bamboo), and *amime* (fishing net). Extensive internal trade within Japan also acquainted sashiko quilters with the designs used by their counterparts in other perfectures and gave rise to many variations of a basic pattern.

For a time during the Edo period, "sumptuary laws" were enacted that legislated simplicity and restraint in the colors and patterns used in clothing. Stripes and plaids met the criteria of the sumptuary laws and were used extensively. New, quintessentially Japanese forms of entertainment, such as the Kabuki theater, also developed during the Edo period. Individual actors popularized distinctively styled textiles, some of which found their way into sashiko designs. For example, the *rokuyata koshi* design originated with the plaid garments that the great actor Danjuro

wore in Kabuki plays to portray the character Rokuyata. Other families of actors, most notably the Nakamura and the Harimaya, created their own "riddle plaids," which were widely imitated by fans. The Kabuki theater's influence on textile design was not restricted to plaids. Other patterns, such as the *kaminari* (thunderbolt) and the *asanoha* (hemp leaf), were also popularized by Kabuki costumes.

In the Meiji period (1868 to 1912), Kabuki plays made their way into the popular culture. Stripes, particularly vertical ones, were popular in the Kabuki costumes of this era. Increased commerce with the United States also brought the influence of designs from American quilting to Japan. Beginning in 1870, Japanese commoners were first allowed to adopt surnames and family crests, and this opportunity provided added impetus for design creativity in sashiko motifs.

With the increased industrialization and affluence of the Taisho (1912 to 1926) and Showa (1926 to 1989) periods, interest in sashiko gradually declined in Japan. By the late 1950s, there seemed to be little interest in the mending technique. However, beginning in the 1970s, sashiko has experienced almost explosive resurgence as a hobby. This interest continues into the present Heisei period.

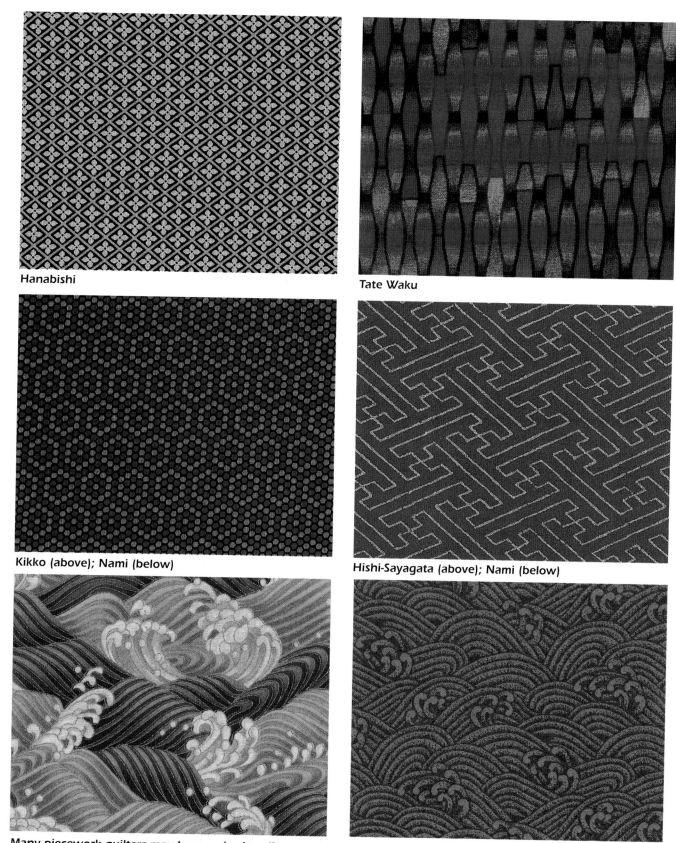

Hanabishi

Tate Waku

Kikko (above); Nami (below)

Hishi-Sayagata (above); Nami (below)

Many piecework quilters may be surprised to discover that the designs on some of their favorite fabric prints are also common sashiko patterns. A representative sample of textiles using sashiko motifs is shown above. The brocade at left shows a typical background weave that was copied in sashiko stitching.

CHAPTER 2

SECRETS of Successful Machine Stitching

Sashiko has never had the popularity it deserves among machine sewers. Unfortunately, most discussions of how to sew sashiko designs by machine rely on the same marking techniques and stitching directions used by hand sewers. This makes stitching sashiko patterns by machine unnecessarily slow and cumbersome and results in a tremendous number of knots to tie. (While a hand sewer can skip between areas of a design by jumping the thread underneath the fabric, the only way to skip between areas when sewing by machine is to cut the thread, tie it off, and start again at the new spot.)

CONTINUOUS STITCHING

The key to realizing that most sashiko designs are readily transferable to a machine environment is to analyze the designs themselves and to ignore completely the traditional methods by which they are drawn and stitched. Most sashiko designs are formed by a continuous line that has been rotated once, twice, or even several times. Any continuous line can, of course, be stitched continuously with a sewing machine. The key to ease in machine stitching is therefore to find the line or lines that form the design and then to mark them in a way that

can be easily followed. Each design shown in this book is accompanied by a color-coded drawing that shows how multiple lines form the design.

THREADS

The sewing technique that has worked best for me is to place the heavier thread in my bobbin, to mark the sashiko design onto the wrong side of the fabric so that I can see it easily, and to sew with the right side of the fabric face down. This technique has advantages beyond the obvious one of simplifying the sewing of the design. The bobbin places far less stress and strain on thread than

Design 3:18 – Kaku-shippo

Specialty threads can add depth and energy to sashiko patterns.

there is when thread is directed through multiple tension dials and the scarf of a needle. Top-stitching-weight thread therefore breaks far less frequently when used in the bobbin, and even exotic threads originally designed to be used in serger loopers can be used to sew sashiko designs. When a removable paper stabilizer is used to "carry" the sashiko design, this technique also allows delicate and nonwashable fabrics to be used for sashiko quilting.

TRANSFERRING PATTERNS

For simple designs, such as straight lines, I often draw the design directly on the interfacing or paper stabilizer that has been affixed to the wrong side of the fabric. For more complex designs, I use iron-transfer pens to replicate the color coding on a plain paper photocopy of the design. If you make a sufficiently dark photocopy, the toner saturates the paper, and the

iron-on transfer ink will "slide" to either side of the photocopied line. As a result, a white line will appear on your interfacing or stabilizer when you iron-on the transfer because none of the transfer ink has been able to permeate the paper where it has been saturated with toner. This white line will be your exact stitching line.

On sturdy fabrics, I fuse white cotton interfacing to the wrong side of fashion fabric and then iron the transfer

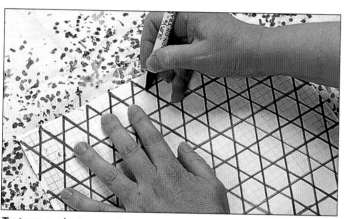

To turn a photocopy into a transfer, drag the transfer pen over the photocopy lines, making sure that the pen is continuously releasing ink. Blot the pen often to maintain a steady ink flow.

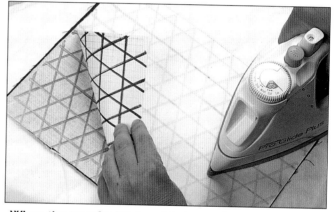

When the transfer ink has dried, transfer the color to the white interfacing or temporary stabilizer with an ordinary iron. Always protect your cover with an old cloth to absorb stray ink.

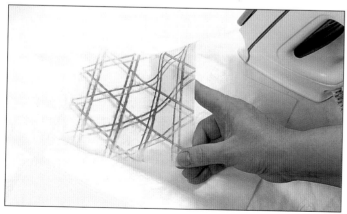

When using temporary stabilizer, transfer the pattern to the stabilizer before tacking it to the wrong side of the fashion fabric. The stabilizer will release easily from the teflon sheet and be ready to adhere to the fashion fabric.

Tack the stabilizer to the wrong side of the fabric and stitch the pattern on the white line. Completely remove the stabilizer by tearing away portions in between the stitching lines. The stabilizer should remove completely.

on to this interfacing. On sheer or delicate fabrics, I first iron the transfer on to a temporary stabilizer whose "sticky" side is placed against a teflon ironing sheet. I can then "tack" the temporary stabilizer to the fashion fabric at a much lower temperature than was necessary to transfer the color-coded design. Using a lower temperature makes the "temporary" sta-

Turn screw to right (clockwise) to increase tension and to the left (counterclockwise) to decrease tension.

bilizer much easier to remove. The photos on page 15 show the steps in preparing and marking permanent interfacing and temporary stabilizer.

Always place an old pressing cloth on your ironing board under any project

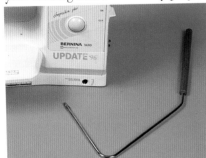

Knee lifter attachment

that uses iron-transfer pens. Some of the ink will migrate whenever the surface of the fabric is heated, and you don't want to stain a "good" ironing board cover.

Note: All projects require an iron, scissors, and a hand sewing needle (to pull threads through to the interfaced side to be knotted).

Sharp corners result from properly balanced tension. If your bobbin thread rounds out at the corner, your bobbin tension is too tight.

BALANCING STITCHES

Once the design is successfully transferred to the interfacing or temporary stabilizer on the wrong side of the fashion fabric, the next step is to balance your stitch so that the bobbin thread (which will end up on the right side of the fashion fabric) forms distinct stitches. To achieve such a balance between needle and bobbin tensions, you will probably need both to loosen your bobbin tension and to tighten your needle tension. The photo

at far left shows how to adjust the tension screw in common types of bobbin cases.

When your tension is properly balanced, the bobbin thread will actually "dive" into the fashion fabric, even showing a little on the interfaced side of the fabric. See good stitch photo samples below.

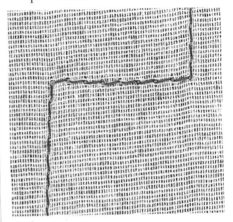

When tension is properly balanced, you will see a small bit of the bobbin thread peeking through on the interfaced side.

HELPFUL MACHINE FEATURES

Machines that have a "needle down" setting have a definite advantage when it comes to sewing curves. In fact, some of the tightest curve

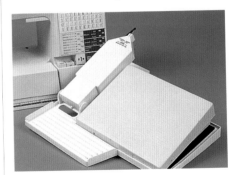

Foot pedal attachment

designs (such as *kasumi* or the "mist" pattern in design 2:9) may be virtually impossible to sew without this feature because the fabric has to be rotated so much after each stitch. Machines that have a "no-hands" presser foot lifter also speed up sewing considerably because they let you use both hands to turn your fabric even as your presser foot is being lifted. Machines without this advantage can be converted with a foot-pedal attachment now available. Finally, a low-bobbin indicator light may also be a convenience, especially for unlined projects where you don't want any avoidable knots.

Design 3:17 – Yabane

Machine accessories can also make your stitching easier and more accurate. An "open-toe" or clear applique foot allows you to see the marked stitching line completely. Seam guide attachments, which are particularly useful if you have both left and right

versions, simplify marking simple designs and help you keep sewn lines parallel to each other.

In order to tackle the designs that involve a pivot or double stitching, you will need to learn how to calibrate your stitch to the length of the shortest line segment in the design. I generally draw my designs on a ¼" grid (6 mm), which corresponds to a stitch length of "8" (stitches per inch) on American machines or approximately a "3" (millimeter-long stitch) on European machines. To test the setting, drop your needle in the exact beginning of an example of the shortest line segment on your design and sew to the end, seeing if your last stitch occurred at the exact end of the line segment. If you find that the "8" or "3" stitch length does not correspond exactly to the shortest line segment on a design, try shortening or lengthening your stitch slightly if you have a variable-stitch-length feature on your machine.

If your machine has only a few pre-programmed settings, experiment with enlarging or reducing the design slightly on a photocopier until you get a good match. The idea is for you to be able to hit the exact beginning and the exact end of a line segment without having to resort to turning your hand wheel manually. Not only will such manual turning slow down

stitching, but it can damage the timing in highly computerized machines.

PRACTICE STRATEGIES

You will probably want to gain some experience in sewing sashiko in this manner before tackling a full-blown project. The designs in the pattern dictionary (see pages 88 - 142) have been grouped by the stitching technique required. Straight line designs are presented first, then curves, then straight lines with pivots, then curves with pivots, then straight lines with pivots and double stitching, then curves with pivots and double stitching. Within each of these groups, designs generally progress in complexity. Designs that use the same basic line have also been grouped together so that you can reinforce your practice on a given type of line. The projects on pages 22 - 87 illustrate some of the many uses for these experimental rectangles once they have served their original purpose of perfecting your stitching technique.

LEARNING TO SEE SASHIKO DESIGNS

When I teach sashiko, I lead my students through a carefully planned series of designs, not only to help them gain experience with curves and in calibrating stitch length, but also to help them see how designs are

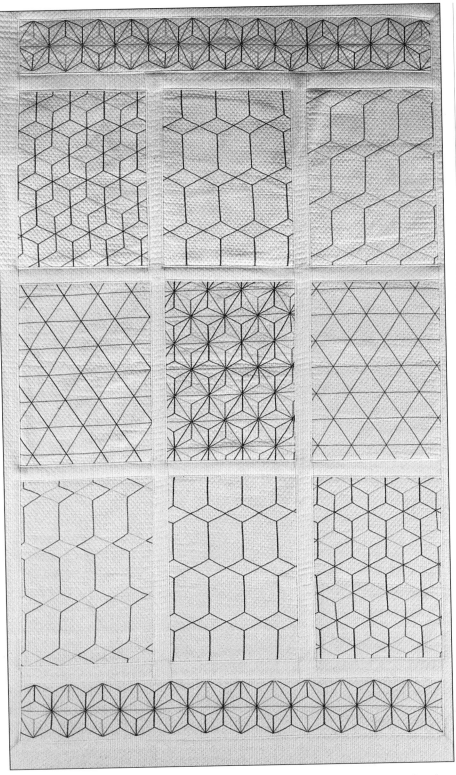

The crib quilt above and the wall hanging at right are good projects to develop your sense of how sashiko designs build upon each other. See pages 69 and 75 for project instructions.

formed. The experience gained in "seeing" the basic line that forms a particular sashiko design assists in analyzing other sashiko designs as well as designs from many other cultures and eras (Art Deco, for example).

In addition, some sashiko designs are formed when other sashiko designs are layered on top of one another in much the same way that *kanji* forms a new word by placing two component words on top of each other. For example, the *kanji* ideograph for prisoner (囚) is formed when the ideograph for enclosure (囗) is placed over the ideograph for man (人). In this same manner, the *asanoha* (hemp leaf) design is formed when the *uroko* (fish scales) design is overlaid on the *tsumiki* (building blocks) design. The *tsumiki* design is itself formed by two offset and overlaid *kasane-kikko* (overlapping tortoiseshells) designs. In a similar manner, two offset and rotated *amime* (fishing net) or *chidori* (plovers) patterns combine to produce the *toridasuki* (interlaced circle of two birds) pattern.

The crib quilt (page 75) and the small wall hanging (page 69) were designed as teaching tools to illustrate these concepts. Even if you choose not to make these projects, reviewing the explanations that follow while looking at a photo of the finished project and at the color-coded illustrations of the designs can help you understand how new designs are formed.

In the crib quilt, the design progression begins at opposite corners of the quilt. The upper right and the lower left rectangles, sewn in blue and yellow thread, both show the kasane kikko pattern, but each uses a different set of mirror-imaged lines to form the pattern, an example of how the same design can often be drawn more than one way. The middle blocks on both the upper and lower rows (sewn in red and green) repeat the same set of lines that were used to form kasane kikko in the beginning rectangle on that row. However, the lines' relative position within the rectangle has been changed, allowing the two blocks to be overlaid to produce the tsumiki pattern, which is shown in blue, yellow, red, and green thread in the lower right and upper left corners. The final step in the design is to add the lines from uroko (stitched in orange, purple, and pink thread) in both left and right blocks of the middle row. When the uroko lines are superimposed on the tsumiki pattern, the asanoha design is formed. This is shown in the center block, which is sewn in all seven colors. Single, linked asanoha designs also form the small border insets at both top and bottom of the quilt.

In the square wall hanging project, the design progression again begins at opposite corners of the quilt. The upper right rectangle, sewn in blue and yellow thread, shows the *chidori* pattern. The lower left rectangle, also sewn in blue and yellow thread, shows the *amine* pattern. The middle blocks on both the upper and lower rows (sewn in red and green) restate the *chidori* and *amine* designs, but subtly transform them, either by rotating or off-setting the original design. Rotating and offsetting the original design allows these two blocks to be overlaid to produce the *toridasuki* pattern, which is shown in blue, yellow, red, and green thread in the lower right and upper left corners. The final step in the design is to add the semicircles (stitched in purple and pink thread) in both left and right

Figure A

Figure B

shown in red. A line that involves both mirror imaging and rotation (usually resulting in movement of 270 degrees) is shown in green. Additional lines are shown in other colors.

This color coding convention leads to a helpful rule for sewing sashiko designs: if you complete stitching all identically colored lines before proceeding to stitch another color of lines, you will allow any embedded designs in your pattern to emerge as you sew.

TIPS FOR SUCCESS

Within a set of identical, parallel lines (those shown in the same color), **stitch from the center out.** This helps the appearance of your finished product if you are using a seam gauge attachment on your machine foot to help you sew parallel lines, and you have happened to set it just a little more or a little less than the actual distance between the lines. Starting at the center and working out in both directions minimizes any discrepancy between your pattern and your actual sewn lines.

Identify the "sweet spots" in the design and make sure that you hit them every time, even if you have to depart from your pattern slightly. The sweet spots are intersection points or inflection points. People viewing your finished product will not be readily

blocks of the middle row. When these semicircles are superimposed on the *toridasuki* pattern, the *hanmaru* design is formed. This is shown in the center block, which is sewn in all six colors.

COLOR CODING

I have used a consistent color-coding method in the designs to help make their pattern formation clear. The basic design line is shown in black. A mirror image of this same line is shown in blue. A rotation of the line (usually 90 degrees or 60 degrees) is able to tell if all your curves really have the same arc or if all your lines are really straight. However, they can easily see an "owie" when multiple lines (that are supposed to converge at one point) miss their target. They may also notice a gap where two lines should meet or an overlap where lines should just touch. Figure A uses a dotted yellow line to show the inflection points in the *kaku-shippo* design. The dotted orange line in Figure B shows where the primary and secondary intersection points occur in the *shippo* design. Some sashiko designs have inflection points as well as intersection points. The human eye will more readily notice that all the stitched lines don't inflect along the same implied line, than it will notice if all the lines aren't the same distance apart.

Sew first those lines that define the boundaries of the design. Often these are horizontal or vertical lines. However, they may be on the diagonal in certain designs. For example, in the most complex variant of the kaku-shippo, the primary defining lines are straight diagonal lines. (See the black and red lines in design 3:19.) Once these lines are sewn, they define the intersection point that all the other lines must hit. Two sets of secondary defining lines also exist in this example: once sewn, they define the inflection points. (See the orange and green pair of lines and the purple and yellow pair of lines in design 3:19.)

Finally, and most important, look for s-curves in the design. And when given a choice between various possible s-curves to sew, always sew the largest. For example, all the instructions that I have found in publications for the *shippo* design plot the sewing pattern for the smaller set of s-curves. This sewing plan makes a lot of sense for hand sewing, but none at all for machine sewing. It is much harder to achieve a good-looking product when sewing these tighter curves by machine than it is when sewing the large s-curves that I show in design 2:3. S-curves may exist in straight line/pivot variants as well as curved lines. For example, the pairs of lines in the *kaku-shippo* pattern mentioned in the paragraph above are the largest s-curves in that design. The pivoting lines on the interior of these defining lines form a series of ever-smaller s-curves.

If you run out of thread when stitching, or if you need to rip out a small section because your stitching is not acceptable, simply pull the stitches out from the underside back far enough so that you have enough loose thread to tie a good stout knot. I always tie a square knot to secure the thread close to the fabric and then tie a half hitch knot as close to the surface of the fabric as is possible. Inserting a sewing needle into the half hitch as it is being drawn closed helps keep the knot from tightening prematurely.

ZEN AND THE ART OF STITCHING SASHIKO BY MACHINE

Although a fair amount of time is required to prepare materials to be sewn by the color-coded, upside-down method that I describe in this book, the actual sewing process itself becomes pure pleasure. As I follow the colored lines, I often find that I become completely, harmoniously focused on the rhythm of my hands pivoting the cloth and of my foot and knee operating the presser-foot lifter and machine speed control. I feel as though I become one with the essence of the design as I bring it to life with fabric and thread. Perhaps if motorcycle maintenance can be a means of Zen meditation, so can sewing sashiko by machine!

 CHAPTER 3

SASHIKO PROJECTS

Sampler Table Runner

Eighteen rectangles from the pattern dictionary make a spectacular table runner. You can use pur-chased extra-wide double-fold bias tape to finish the edges of the runner or you can make your own binding, as described here. The technique to apply the binding described here produces a folded miter finish for the corners of the runner. Chose any 18 designs that strike your fancy!

MATERIALS + TOOLS

3 yards (2.7 m) 36" (91 cm) or wider fashion fabric

3 yards (2.7 m) of lining fabric

50 mm (2" wide) bias tape maker (optional, but very helpful)

1¼ yards (1.12 m) white cotton fusible interfacing

4 or 5 spools of top-stitching-weight thread for sashiko

Regular sewing thread

Photocopies of sashiko patterns

Iron-on transfer pens

INSTRUCTIONS

■**1**■ Cut out 18 rectangles measuring 8½ x 11" (22 x 28 cm) from the fashion fabric. Cut out 16 short piecing strips on straight of grain for joining. Cut out one strip of fashion fabric measuring 99" long x 2" wide, cut on straight of grain for joining. Cut enough 3¼"-wide (8.25 cm) fabric strips on the straight of the grain to make a 7-yard length for the binding.

■**2**■ Photocopy the desired sashiko patterns from the dictionary, ink with iron-on transfer pens, and let dry. Apply the rectangle of fusible interfacing (glue side down) to the wrong side of the rectangles of fashion fabric according to manufacturer's directions. Apply the sashiko design to the interfaced side of the rectangles and stitch.

■**3**■. Abut the 18 rectangles together, face up, as you want them to appear when they are permanently stitched together. Working with one rectangle at a time, lay a short piecing strip right side down against the 8½"

top of each of the rectangles that has another rectangle above it, matching raw edges. Pin and stitch. Press seam toward piecing strip.

■**4**■ After sewing each seam, place the rectangle back on the table in its original position, then flip it over on top of the rectangle above it so that the other raw edge of the short piecing strip is now even with the bottom 8½" raw edge of the other rectangle. Pin and stitch. Press seam toward piecing strip. When you have completed stitching all 16 of the short piecing strips, you should have two 99 x 8½" (2.5 m x 22 cm) sets of rectangles sewn together.

■**5**■ Lay the 99" strip right side down against the 99" center side of one of the strips of rectangles, matching raw edges. Pin and stitch. Press seam toward piecing strip. Lay the pieced strip back in its original place, then flip it over the other pieced strip so that the other 99" raw edge of the piecing strip is now even with the center raw edge of the other pieced strip. Pin and stitch. Press seam toward piecing strip.

■**6**■ Stitch 3¼"-wide strips together until you have a continuous piece that totals 7 yards. If you have a 50 mm (2" wide) bias tape maker, use it to turn ⅝" (16 mm) under on each long edge of the 60" strip to form a 2"-wide strip. If you don't have a bias tape maker, press up a ⅝" "hem" on each long side of the 7-yard strip.

■**7**■ Fold the 7-yard strip in half lengthwise, favoring the bottom edge so that it extends ⅛" (3 mm) beyond the top edge. Layer your runner together with the lining right side

down and the sashiko rectangles right side up on top. Baste all around the edges of the runner.

■**8**■ Open up the tape and fold back ½" (13 mm) across one short end. Place that end even with the seam line for the piecing strip at the center bottom of the runner with right sides together and raw edges even. The line that was formed when one side of the strip was pressed under ⅝" will now be on the ⅝" stitching line for the rectangle.

■**9**■ Sew on the line formed in step 8, stopping ⅝" from the corner of the rectangle; backstitch to secure stitching. Lift up the strip and refold against the rectangle so that the area you just sewed is folded back against itself, forming a triangle. Square off the top of the strip against the corner of the rectangle. Resume stitching ⅝" out from the corner on the ⅝" pressed hem line and continue until you are within ⅝" of the next corner.

■**10**■ Repeat step 9 for each edge of the runner until you are back at your initial starting point. Overlap the edge of the binding by ½" and trim off excess binding. Turn the binding right side out, folding it around the edge of the runner. Pin in place on the top side in the "ditch" between the binding and the runner, making sure that the binding on the underside extends far enough to be caught when you "stitch in the ditch" from the top side. Stitch in the ditch.

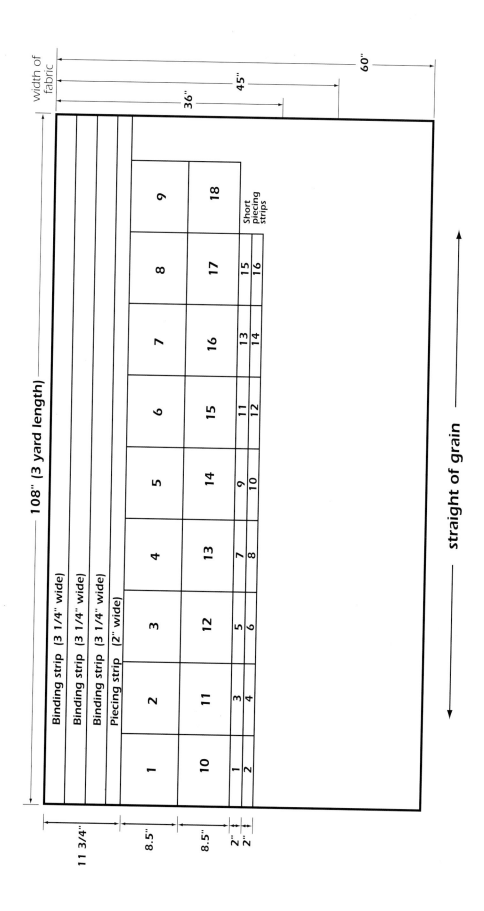

Width of fabric

108" (3 yard length)

Binding strip (3 1/4" wide)
Binding strip (3 1/4" wide)
Binding strip (3 1/4" wide)
Piecing strip (2" wide)

60"
45"
36"

1	2	3	4	5	6	7	8	9
10	11	12	13	14	15	16	17	18
1	5	7	9	11	13	15		
2	6	8	10	12	14	16		
3								
4								

Short piecing strips

11 3/4"
8.5"
8.5"
2"
2"

straight of grain

25

Hot Pads

A single rectangle is just the right size for a hot pad. You can use purchased extra-wide double-fold bias tape to finish the edges of each rectangle or you can make your own binding, as described here. The technique to apply the binding described here produces a folded miter finish for the corners of the rectangle. If desired, place dried herbs between the sashiko top and the batting so that their aroma is released whenever a hot pot is placed on the pad.

MATERIALS + TOOLS

8½ x 11" (22 x 28 cm) rectangle of fashion fabric (makes one pad)

Strip of fashion fabric measuring 45 long x 3¼" wide (1.14 m x 8.25 cm), cut on straight of grain, for binding

8½ x 11" rectangle of printed cotton for bottom of hot pad (¼ yard will make four)

50 mm (2" wide) bias tape maker (optional, but very helpful)

1 or 2 (depending on desired thickness) 8½ x 11" rectangles of cotton batting

8½ x 11" rectangle of white cotton fusible interfacing

Top-stitching-weight thread for sashiko

Regular sewing thread

Photocopies of sashiko patterns

Iron-on transfer pens

INSTRUCTIONS

■**1**■ Photocopy the desired sashiko pattern from the dictionary, ink with iron-on transfer pens, and let dry. Apply the rectangle of fusible interfacing (glue side down) to the wrong side of the rectangle of fashion fabric according to manufacturer's directions. Apply the sashiko design to the interfaced side of the rectangle and stitch.

■**2**■ If you have a 50 mm (2" wide) bias tape maker, use it to turn ⅝" (16 mm) under on each long edge of the 45" strip to produce a 2"-wide strip. If you don't have a bias tape maker, press up a ⅝" "hem" on each long side of the 45" strip. Fold the 45" strip in half lengthwise, favoring the bottom edge so that it extends ⅛" (3 mm) beyond the top edge.

■**3**■ Layer your hot pad together with the lining right side down, the batting in the middle, and the sashiko rectangle right side up on top. Baste around all the edges of the rectangle.

■**4**■ Open up the tape and fold back ½" (13 mm) across one short end. Place that end at the center bottom of the rectangle with right sides together and raw edges even. The line that was formed when one side of the strip was pressed under ⅝" should now be on the ⅝" stitching line for the rectangle.

■**5**■ Sew on the line, stopping ⅝" from the corner of the rectangle; backstitch to secure stitching. Lift up the strip and refold against the rectangle so that the area you just sewed is folded back against itself, forming a tri-angle. Square off the top of the strip against the corner of the rectangle.

■**6**■ Stitch ⅝" out from the corner on the ⅝" pressed hem line and continue until you are within ⅝" of the next corner. Repeat this step for each edge of the hot pad until you are back at your initial starting point. Overlap the edge of the binding by ½" and trim off excess binding.

■**7**■ Turn the binding right side out, folding it around the edge of the hot pad. Pin in place on the top side in the "ditch" between the binding and the hot pad, making sure that the binding on the underside extends far enough to be caught when you stitch in the ditch from the top side. Stitch in the ditch.

Above, design 4:5 – Nowaki; Opposite page, design 5:8, Bishamon

Flange Border Pillows

A *pillow with a flange border is as easy to sew as a regular pillow, yet it looks much more sophisticated and creates a natural area for sashiko embellishment. You can embellish the pillow body with sashiko and leave the flange area plain or vice versa. Sew companion pillows in unexpected color combinations for an avant-garde look.*

MATERIALS + TOOLS

Square pillow form

½ yard (.45 m) of 45" (1.14 m) fashion fabric for each pillow (do not trim)

White cotton fusible interfacing cut either in a square the same dimensions as the pillow form (if you plan to embellish the pillow's body area) or in a hollow square 3" to 4" (7.5 to 10 cm) larger than the pillow form (if you plan to embellish the flange area)

Photocopies of chosen sashiko designs

Iron-on transfer pens

Pearl cotton thread for sashiko

Regular thread

PROJECT PLANNING

You will need fabric that is 3" to 4" (7.5 to 10 cm) wider than the dimensions of your pillow form. A 14" (36 cm) pillow is the maximum that can be used with 18"-long (46 cm) fabric (½ yard, .45 m). You want a tight fit for the pillow to show the flange to best advantage, so don't allow any "ease" in fitting the pillow form.

INSTRUCTIONS

■**1**■ Mark a square that has the same dimensions as the pillow form and mark another, larger square surrounding the first square that represents the dimensions of the pillow form plus the flange width with chalk in the center of the wrong side of the fabric. Make sure that you have enough fabric for a seam allowance beyond this square along both raw edges.

■**2**■ Apply interfacing on the wrong side of the fabric either to smaller square (if your sashiko will be on the pillow body) or to the "frame" formed

Design 7:6 — Yotsugumi Hishi

between the two squares (if your sashiko will be on the flange).

■ **3** ■ Choose a suitable design and make a photocopy. Cut the photocopy to the appropriate size if sewing only on the flange. Ink the photocopy and let dry. Transfer the designs to the interfacing, overlapping where necessary.

■ **4** ■ Stitch the sashiko design. Fold the selvage edges of the fabric, wrong sides together, back 2" (5 cm) to form a hem for the back opening of the pillow. Pin and stitch, then press.

■ **5** ■ Place the fabric, sashiko side up, on a flat work surface. Fold the fabric, right sides together so that only the area of the pillow and the flange is face down, on the work surface and the two hemmed edges are overlapping in back. Pin the raw edges together and stitch. Press seams open and trim seam allowance in corners. Turn to right side.

■ **6** ■ Top-stitch on right side in a square that has the same dimension as the pillow form, using the edge of the sashiko as a guide. (Hint: Set your machine guide arm at the same distance from the finished edge of the fabric that the flange is wide.) Insert pillow.

Design 4:7 — Fuji

Design 3:11 — Inazuma

Above: Design 1:6 — Nakumura Koshi
Right: Design 3:14 — Hishi-sayagata

Sashiko Throw Pillows

Pillows make a great showcase for specialty designs and threads, and this slipcover style allows you to change pillow styles as often as you like.

MATERIALS + TOOLS

Square pillow form

½ yard (.45 m) 45" (1.14 m) fashion fabric for each pillow (covers up to 16", 41 cm, throw pillow)

½ yard 45" white cotton fusible interfacing (makes two square throw pillows)

Four tassels

Various colors of top-stitching-weight thread to match tassel

Regular sewing thread

Crochet hook or similar device to pull tassel ends through pillow

Photocopies of sashiko designs

Iron-on transfer pens

INSTRUCTIONS

■ **1** ■ Measure your square pillow from the center of one side to the center of the other side to determine how large your sashiko embellished area will need to be. (The stated dimensions of the pillow refer only to the distance between its flat outside boundaries. They don't allow for the "rise," or the height, of the pillow. For example, many 16", 41 cm, pillows will actually measure 17", 43 cm, when the "rise" is taken into account.)

■ **2** ■ Add 1" (2.5 cm) to your measurement and cut the white cotton interfacing to a square this size. (The extra inch is to allow for the sashiko stitching to "pull up" your fabric slightly, particularly if you are making a design with many lines of stitching.) Center this square, glue side down on the wrong side of your fabric. Do not trim your fabric! You will use the entire 45" width of the fabric in this project. Fuse the interfacing into place.

■ **3** ■ Ink the photocopy of the sashiko design and let it dry. Transfer the design to the interfacing, overlapping the design as you move the photocopy until the entire area of the interfacing is marked. Sew the sashiko design.

■ **4** ■ Fold the selvage edges of the fabric, wrong sides together, back 2" (5 cm) to form a hem for the back opening of the pillow. Pin and stitch, then press.

■ **5** ■ Place the fabric, sashiko side up on a work surface. Fold the fabric with right sides together so that only the sashiko stitching is face down on the work surface and the two hemmed edges are overlapping in back. Pin the raw edges together and machine baste. Turn right side out.

■ **6** ■ Try the cover on your pillow and note how much additional fabric (if any) should be taken up in the seam to get a tight fit across the pillow from seam to seam. Also check to see if there's too much slack across the other side of the pillow (from folded

Above: Design 6:1 — Matsunami
Right: Designs 3:20 — Untitled Hokusai #4 (top) and 6:7 — Kiku (bottom)

side to folded side). If so, fold your fabric farther back to make the pillow front smaller.

■ **7** ■ Turn the pillow back wrong side out. If you need to decrease the width of the pillow cover from folded side to folded side, rip out your basting and refold the fabric so that less is left facing down on the table and the amount of the overlap is increased. Re-pin. If you need to decrease the width of the pillow cover from sewn side to sewn side, stitch a deeper seam, using the marks left by the basting to gauge the additional depth neded. Sew the top and bottom seams, stopping ⅛" (3 mm) shy of the corner.

Place a tassel snugly in the corner of the inside-out pillow cover. Use a crochet hook or similar device to pull the large loop of the tassel through at the corner. Secure in place with hand stitches. Repeat for the other corners. Turn the cover right side out and insert pillow.

Comforter or Duvet Cover

Treat yourself to a comforter or duvet cover made from sashiko rectangles. This project is easier than you might think and gives you a great excuse to stitch a variety of patterns.

PROJECT PLANNING

Full/Queen: Most common dimensions for quilt or comforter are 86 x 86" (2.18 m). You will need a total of 63 sashiko rectangles, arranged 9 across and 7 down. You will sew the rectangles together horizontally first, using eight 2"-wide (5 cm) strips (cut on lengthwise grain of fabric) that are 76.5" (1.94 m) long. You will then cut this strip apart between the rectangles and sew the resulting long strips together using six 2"-wide strips (cut on lengthwise grain of fabric) that are 77" (1.95 m) long. When the seam allowances are taken into account, your resulting piece will have finished dimensions of 76.5" wide x 77" long. To get the desired 86 x 86" final dimension, cut two side border pieces and two top/bottom border pieces as indicated in the cutting diagram, then miter the corners of these as you sew them to the sashiko piece. Your backing fabric for the quilt/duvet cover needs to be 87" wide and 87" long.

MATERIALS AND TOOLS

6 yards (5.4 m) fashion fabric for the top

5 yards (4.5 m) of fabric for the lining

4⅔ yards (4.2 m) 45" wide (1.14 m) white cotton fusible interfacing

10 to 12 spools of top-stitching weight thread for sashiko

Regular sewing thread

Photocopies of sashiko patterns

Iron-on transfer pens

INSTRUCTIONS

■1■ Cut out the fashion fabric according to cutting diagram on page 65. Cut out 13 rows of 8½ x 11" (20 x 28 cm) rectangles (5 rectangles to a row) of interfacing with the 11" side on the lengthwise grain. Chose and photocopy a variety of sashiko designs for the 63 rectangles. Ink the photocopies and let them dry. Transfer the designs to the interfacing and sew the sashiko designs.

■2■ Place nine rectangles face up on a table so that they abut each other along their 11" (28 cm) sides to form a 76.5" wide 76.5) row. This will be lowest horizontal row on the duvet cover.

■3■ Pin one 76.5" strip in place face down on the upper edge of the rectangles. Sew a ½" (13 mm) seam and press the seam so that the rectangle is flat rather than turned back on itself. Return the rectangles and the strip to the table so that the rectangles are once again face up and the sewn strip is at the top.

■4■ Lay the next row of nine rectangles face up on the table so that they are abutting each other along their 11" sides. Flip the part that you have already sewn together so that you are placing the raw edge of the sewn strip right side down on the lower edge of the nine new rectangles. Pin and sew a ½" seam. Press the seam so that the rectangles are flat rather than turned back on themselves.

■5■ Return your work to the table so that the rectangles are face up and the sewn strip is in the middle of the two sets of rectangles. Be

Detail of pattern 3:23, Inozuma. See page 116 in the Pattern Dictionary.

Duvet Cover

1	2	3	4	5	6	7
8	9	10	11	12	13	14
15	16	17	18	19	20	21
22	23	24	25	26	27	28
29	30	31	32	33	34	35
36	37	38	39	40		
41	42	43	44	45		
46	47	48	49	50		
51	52	53	54	55		
56	57	58	59	60		
61	62	63	64	65		

208"

Cut six 2" wide strips here

77"

←12"→

87"

Cut four 10 1/2" wide strips here

Cut eight 2" wide strips here

76 1/2"

←42"→   ←16"→

←60"→

sure that your bottom row is at the bottom. Pin a second 76.5" strip in place face down on the upper edge of the upper row of rectangles. Sew a 1/2" seam and press the seam so that the rectangle is flat rather than turned back on itself. Repeat this step until strips are sewn between all seven rows.

■6■ Cut between the rectangles so that you are left with nine 77" long strips of rectangles that have been joined together top and bottom. Place the left most strip of rectangles face up on a table and pin one of the 77" strips right side down along its right side. Sew a ½" seam and press the seam so that all rectangles are flat rather than turned back on themselves.

■7■ Lay your second left most strip of rectangles face up on the table. Flip the part that you have already sewn so that you are placing the raw edge of the sewn strip right side down on the left most edge of the seven new rectangles. Pin and sew a ½" seam. Press the seam so that the rectangles are flat rather than turned back on themselves.

■8■ Return your work to the table so that the rectangles face up and the newly sewn strip is in the middle of the two strips of rectangles. Be sure that your left most row is to the far left. Pin a second 77" strip in place face down on the right edge of the right row of rectangles. Sew a ½" seam and press the seam so that the rectangle is flat rather than turned back on itself. Repeat these steps until strips are sewn between all nine strips of rectangles.

■9■ Attach and miter the border pieces, then line your cover.

Gift Wrap Cloths

The traditional Japanese wrapping cloth takes on an elegant form when created from silk fabrics and shimmering threads. Replacing both paper and bow, wrapping cloths take up little space and can be reused year after year. The designs on the packages can even hint at their contents. For example, the measuring box design wraps a present of measuring cups, spoons, and other kitchen utensils for a newlywed, while the clove and mandarin orange flower patterns hint at a gift of spiced cider mix.

MATERIALS + TOOLS

Fabric (amount depends on the box size, but generally 1 yard, .9 m, for medium-size boxes and 1¼ yard, 1.1 m, for large boxes)

Same amount of lining, if lining is desired

Enough nonweft insertion nylon tricot interfacing that fuses on a "silk" setting to cover areas that will be stitched with sashiko, if making a lined cloth

Packet or two of temporary, tear-away, white paper iron-on stabilizer, depending on how much of the surface of the cloth is stitched with sashiko, if making an unlined cloth

Photocopies of chosen sashiko designs

Iron-on transfer pens

Heavy metallic thread for sashiko

Regular thread

PROJECT PLANNING

Wrapping cloths can be lined or unlined. If you choose to line the wrapping cloth, you can use a perma-nent interfacing to support the sashiko stitching because it will be hidden. The raw edges of the fabric will also be enclosed in the seam that sews the lining and outer fabric together. When the package is wrapped, the lining will show only on the reverse side of the "bow" on top. All of the two-tone wrapping cloths in the photos are lined. If you make an unlined version, you will need to use a temporary, iron-on paper stabilizer that you can remove after the sashiko design is sewn. To prevent ravelling, the edges of the cloth will need to be finished with a serger rolled hem or another narrow hem finish. The pale green wrapping cloth with the *kagome* design is unlined with a serger rolled hem finish in the same metallic thread used for the sashiko stitching.

To have the "bow" fit exactly on the top of the box, scale your wrapping cloth to the package you intend to wrap. Run a tape measure under the

Design 1:11–Kagome

Design 6:6–Take

Figure 1

bottom of the box and measure the total distance around both sides. Boxes that appear to be "square" often are not. (See Figure 1.) If you intend to line the wrapping cloth, add 1" (2.5 cm) and two seam allowances to the larger measurement. If you intend to leave the wrapping cloth unlined, add 1" plus twice the hem allowance to the larger measurement. To tie the wrapping cloth properly, the fabric should always be exactly square, even if your package is not. Boxes that appear very different will often yield the same measurement, so the wrapping cloths are more interchangeable than one might think.

ALTERNATIVES TO ALL OVER STITCHING

Designs can be sewn all over or the wrapping can be embellished

selectively. To mark the area of the wrapping cloth where the sashiko will go, place the trimmed wrapping cloth fabric face down on a work surface. Place the box in the exact center of the fabric, with the sides of the box facing the corners of the fabric. Draw a chalk line on the fabric around the bottom of the box (shown as section "A" on the diagram). Then tip the box over on its side and chalk that outline on the fabric (shown as section "B" on the diagram). Tip the box again to mark the outline of the top of the box (shown as section "C").

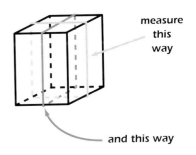

measure this way

and this way

Left, design 3:15–Matsukawa-bishi; right, design 3:4–Juji

40

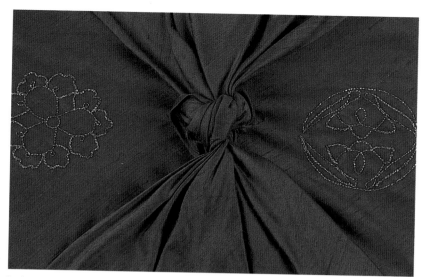

Left, design 6:10–Choji; right, design 6:9–Tachibana

Alternatives to All-over Stitching

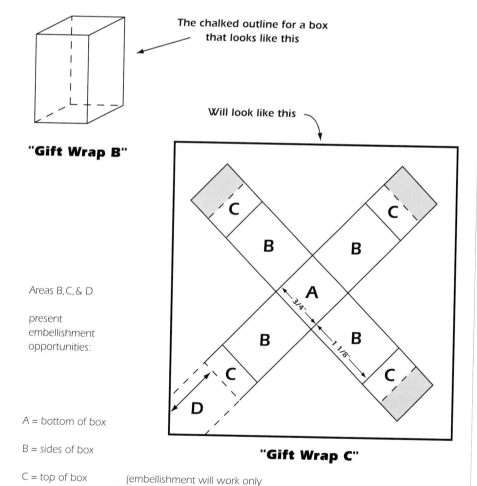

The chalked outline for a box that looks like this

"Gift Wrap B"

Will look like this

Areas B, C, & D

present
embellishment
opportunities:

"Gift Wrap C"

A = bottom of box

B = sides of box

C = top of box

(embellishment will work only
on first half: cross-hatched
area will be covered up or in knot)

D = triangular flap (only one will show)

INSTRUCTIONS

■ **1** ■ Cut the fabric and lining separately. If applying selective embellishment rather than an overall design, on the wrong side of the outer fabric, mark the areas in which interfacing or stabilizer needs to be applied to support the sashiko stitching. Choose a suitable design, make a photocopy, and cut to the appropriate size. Ink the photocopy and let it dry.

■ **2** ■ If making the unlined version, transfer the design from the photocopy to the stabilizer using a teflon pressing sheet. Lightly tack the stabilizer to the wrong side of the outer fabric in the needed areas. If making the lined version, apply the interfacing according to manufacturer's directions in the needed areas and then transfer the design to the interfacing. Stitch the sashiko design.

■ **3** ■ If making the unlined version, remove the stabilizer. Hem all four sides. If making the lined version, place right sides of the lining and upper fabric together. Pin and stitch together, leaving an opening along the longer straight side to turn. Press seams open and trim seam allowance in corners. Turn to right side. Slipstitch the opening closed.

Pillow Shams

This project makes a pair of pillow shams with a 2 1/2" (5 cm) flange border around the edge which is suitable for any 2"-wide (5 cm) sashiko border design, while the center of the pillow is suitable for a larger motif (approximately 7", 18 cm).

MATERIALS + TOOLS

2¾ (2.5 m) yards of 54"-60"-wide (1.37-1.52 m) fabric

¾ yard (.67 m) of 45"-wide (1.14 m) white cotton fusible interfacing

Photocopies of chosen sashiko designs

Iron-on transfer pens

Heavy thread for sashiko

Regular thread

INSTRUCTIONS

■ **1** ■ Cut the fabric into two pieces, each measuring 96" long by 26" wide (2.43 x .66 m). From the interfacing, cut six 2½"-wide (6.4 cm) strips on the cross-grain. Trim four of them to 42½" long. Cut the remaining two strips into two pieces each that are 20½" long. Also cut two squares that are slightly larger than the center motif. (Mine were 7" square.) See cutting layout on page 44.

■ **2** ■ Draw a chalk line down the center of one of the 96"-long pieces of fabric on its wrong side. (This line will be 48", 1.22 m, from each end of the fabric.) Lay the fabric, wrong side up, on a 72" (1.83 m) long work surface and center the chalk line on the center of the work surface.

■ **3** ■ Fold the fabric that hangs over the edge on each side back on the work surface so that it won't pull the rest of the fabric off-grain. Place the

Central motif: design 8:5—Hoya. Border: design 2:7—Toridasuki

Central motif: design 8:6—Genji-Guruma. Border: design 4:1—Seigaiha

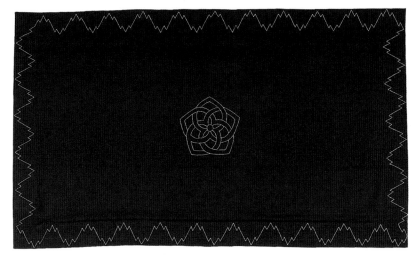

Central motif: design 8:3—Kikyo. Border: design 3:15—Matsukawa-Bishi

square and two long and two short pieces of the 2½" interfacing, glue side down, on the wrong side of the fabric as shown in Figure 1. Pin into place.

■ **4** ■ Fuse the interfacing strips in place, removing the pins from each section before fusing it. Cut the photocopies for the border design into 2¼" (6.7 cm) wide strips to facilitate centering them on the strips of interfacing. Trim the photocopy for the center motif close to the design. Ink the photocopies with the iron-on transfer markers and let dry.

■ **5** ■ Transfer the design from the photocopies to the interfacing using the manufacturer's directions. Stitch the designs.

■ **6** ■ To make the placket on the back of the pillow sham through which the pillow will be inserted, finish both 26"- long raw edges of the fabric so that they won't ravel, then fold back 2" (5 cm) of fabric on each of these edges, wrong sides together, to form a "hem." Press and stitch near the raw edge.

■ **7** ■ Place the fabric right side up on a flat work surface. Fold first one side and then the other up, right sides together, so that only the stitched area is facing down to form a rectangle 43" (1.09 m) long by 26" wide with an overlap of approximately 6" (15 cm).

■ **8** ■ Pin and stitch the 43"-long edges of the sham in a ⅝" (16 mm) seam. Turn to the right side and press. Pin the two layers of the pillow sham together approximately 2½" out from each edge.

■ **9** ■ To make the flange, begin stitching in the middle of one side

2½" away from the edge of the pillow sham. Pivot when you are 2½" away from the next edge of the sham. Continue stitching and pivoting every time that you are 2½" away from the next edge so that you sew a rectangle on the top of the pillow sham. Insert the pillow from the back.

Central motif: design 8:4–Sakura. Border: design 3:12–Sayagata.

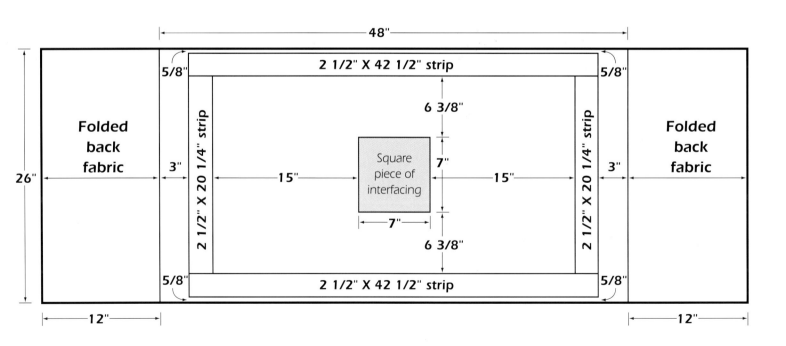

Window Swag

This project makes a swag for a small window (approximately 22" wide x 38" high, 56 x 97 cm). The swag provides a setting to showcase a small sashiko motif such as kakitsubata (design 6:9) on the "drop" on each side.

MATERIALS + TOOLS

2¾ yards (2.5 m) of fashion fabric at least 45" (1.14 m) wide for top side of swag

2¾ yards of fashion fabric at least 45" wide for lining side of swag

Packet of temporary, tear-away, iron-on stabilizer

Photocopies of chosen sashiko designs

Iron-on transfer pens

Heavy thread for sashiko

Regular thread

INSTRUCTIONS

■**1**■. Cut the fabric and lining separately according to the diagram. Choose a design suitable for being stitched in the "drop" of each side of the swag. Make a photocopy and cut to the appropriate size.

■**2**■ Ink the photocopy and let it dry. Transfer the design from the photocopy to the stabilizer using a teflon pressing sheet. Lightly tack the stabilizer to the wrong side of the lining (not to the upper fabric!) in the triangular area along the swag's shorter side. Stitch the sashiko design and remove the stabilizer.

■**3**■ Pin the lining and upper fabrics together with right sides facing. Stitch together, leaving an opening along the longer straight side to turn. Press seams open, trim seam allowance in

corners, and turn to right side. Slipstitch the opening closed.

■**4**■ Fold in loose pleats, thread through hanging brackets, and "plump" until it hangs luxuriously.

Cutting Layout

**Cut one each of upper fabric and of
lining according to diagram**

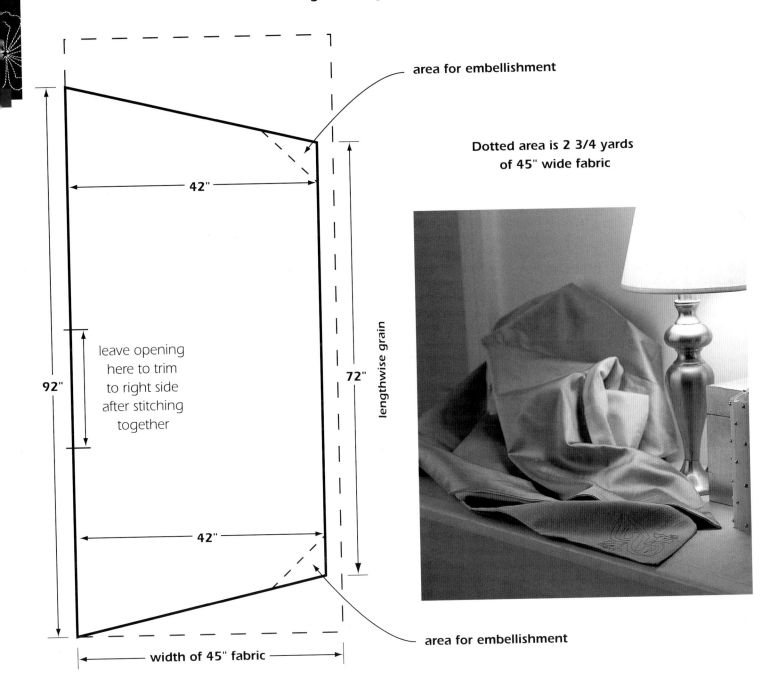

area for embellishment

**Dotted area is 2 3/4 yards
of 45" wide fabric**

42"

72"

92"

lengthwise grain

leave opening
here to trim
to right side
after stitching
together

42"

area for embellishment

width of 45" fabric

Sashiko Hand Towels

Adding a sashiko design to a hand towel takes less than an hour, making this project a wonderful gift idea.

MATERIALS + TOOLS

Purchased plain linen hand towel

Regular thread to match towel

Contrasting top-stitching-weight thread for sashiko

Packet of removable iron-on stablizer

Photocopies of sashiko designs

Iron-on transfer pens

INSTRUCTIONS

■1■. Remove the stitching from the front hem of the towel. Lightly press the hem area so that the fabric lies flat, but so that you can still see the original hem fold line. Measure the depth of the hem from the fold line to the original stitching line, and cut a row of temporary stablizer in this same width. (Note: If the hem of the towel is not wide enough for your chosen sashiko design, simply press a new hem and cut the interfacing to this width.)

■2■ Cut your photocopies to the width of the stablizer, ink them, and let dry. Transfer the design from the photocopy to the stablizer using a teflon pressing sheet. Lightly tack the stablizer to the wrong side of the body (not to the facing!) of the towel in the area between the hem fold and the original stitching line.

■3■ Stitch the sashiko design and remove the stablizer. Press the hem

back in place and stitch to secure. Note: if you can't find plain linen towels to embellish, it's easy to make your own. Simply narrow-hem both raw edges of an 18"-long (46 cm) piece of 40"-wide (1 m) linen or linen-cotton blend fabric. (The selvage edges will be pressed under to become the front and back hems of the towel and the hemmed edges will be the sides.) Press and stitch a 1" (2.5 cm) hem for the back of the towel. Press the desired front hem width (a minimum of 4" is recommended), then follow the steps outlined here.

Design 4:7–Fuji

Summer Table Runner

This project combines the two popular sashiko patterns associated with the summer season—
kagome (woven bamboo) and amine (fishing net)—into an original design for a festive table runner.
Because the runner is narrow, you'll have plenty of leftover fabric to make matching napkins or additional runners to give as gifts.

Designs 2:5— Amine and 1:11— Kagomi

MATERIALS +TOOLS

Fashion fabric 12" (31 cm) wide and at least 20" (51 cm) longer than the length of your table (generally about 3 yards, 2.7 m)

Lining fabric in same dimensions

3 yards of white cotton fusible inter-facing (at least 12" wide)

11 x 17" (28 x 43 cm) photocopies of sashiko design provided

Iron-on transfer pens

Four different colors of topstitching thread for sashiko

Regular thread

Latch hook

Tassels for runner ends, optional

INSTRUCTIONS

■ **1** ■ Cut the fabric and lining separately, starting a taper to a triangular point about 8" from each end. Ink the photocopy and let it dry.

■ **2** ■ Fuse the interfacing to the wrong side of the fashion fabric. Transfer the sashiko design to the interfacing, overlapping the design. Stitch the sashiko design.

■ **3** ■ Pin and stitch the lining and fashion fabrics together with right sides together, leaving an opening along one long straight side to turn.

Press seams open. Trim seam allowance around pivot points. Turn to right side and press.

■ **4** ■ Extend a latch hook from the inside to the outside through the point at each end. Pull the loop of the tassel back through the point of the runner to the inside. Secure in place. Slipstitch the side opening closed.

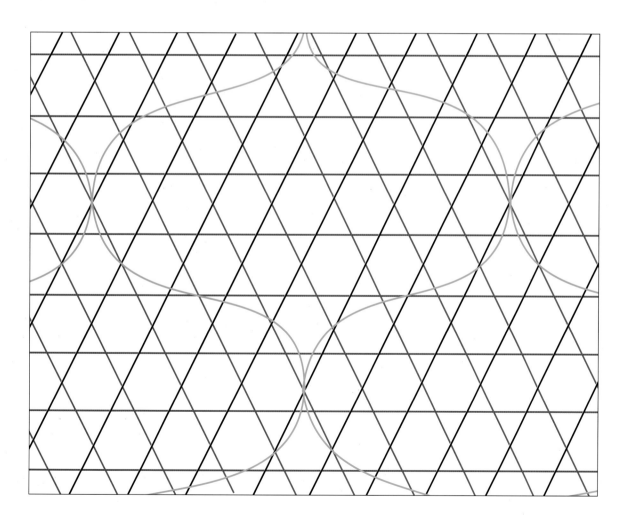

Sashiko Director's Chairs

This project is suitable for any motif that can be continuously sewn from the starting point to the ending point. Since the stitching will be visible from the reverse side, conceal the knot in the hem.

MATERIALS + TOOLS

Director's chairs with removable covers

One package white temporary-fuse, tear-away stabilizer

Top-stitching-weight thread for sashiko

Regular sewing thread

Photocopies of sashiko patterns

Iron-on transfer pens

Above, right side; below, wrong side

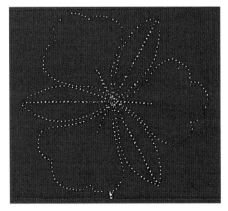

**Far right: Design 4:8–Tessen
Design 4:11–Katabami**

INSTRUCTIONS

■**1**■ Measure the area in between the top and bottom hems of the director's chair back. (This is usually is about 5", 13 cm.) Make photocopies of motif-type designs that will fit into this area. You may need to reduce or enlarge, depending on the selected pattern.

■**2**■ Cut the photocopy to the size of the finished design, ink, and let dry. Transfer the design to the stabilizer with a teflon ironing sheet with the stabilizer's shiny side down next to the teflon sheet. Iron the inked photocopy onto the stabilizer using the heat setting recommended by the iron-on pen's manufacturer. Let the stabilizer cool, and peel it off the teflon sheet.

■**3**■ Reapply the stabilizer to the wrong side of the director's chair cover, using the minimum heat and time necessary to get the stabilizer to attach. (This will make it easier to remove the stabilizer after the stitching is complete.)

■**4**■ Stitch the sashiko design, starting at a point as near as possible to the hem either on top or bottom. After completing the design, tie off the threads in a knot and hide the knotted thread in the hem. Remove the stabilizer.

Doorway Curtain/ Narrow Wall Hanging

The traditional Japanese doorway curtain provided the inspiration for this wall hanging. Designed to be hung in a narrow window at the side of a conventional Western front door, this hanging illustrates an autumn landscape complete with a flock of plovers (chidori) and a hillside of blowing pampas grass (nowaki). If you'd like a second, symmetrical curtain, simply mirror-image your entire design on a second hanging.

PROJECT PLANNING

Measure the width of the window or opening that you wish to cover. Add 2-3" (5-7 cm) for hanging ease and two seam allowances to this measurement. This will be the width of your fabric. Measure the length that you want the curtain to hang. Add 2-3" ease for a casing at the top and one hem allowance for the bottom to this measurement. This will be the length of your fabric.

To make your own original design, cut a rectangle with the dimensions obtained above from pattern tracing pattern. Slide photocopies of various sashiko patterns under the tracing paper until you have created a satisfactory seasonal tableau. Trace the lines from the underlying photocopies on to the paper. Use stripes or checks to connect the various motifs in the design. When you have finalized your design, turn the pattern tracing paper over and darken the lines on the reverse side of the paper. (This step will create a mirror image.) Photocopy both sides.

MATERIALS + TOOLS

Fabric determined in planning step above (generally at least 2 yards, 1.8 m, is needed)

Same amount of lining fabric

Same amount of white cotton fusible interfacing

Photocopies of sashiko design

Iron-on transfer pens

Heavy rayon threads for sashiko

Regular thread

INSTRUCTIONS

■**1**■ Cut the fabric and lining separately. Fuse the interfacing to the wrong side of the fabric.

■**2**■ Make design photocopies and reassemble them into a full-size pattern. Ink the reassembled photocopies and let them dry. Transfer the design to the interfacing and stitch the sashiko design.

■**3**■ Pin the lining and upper fabric together with right sides facing and stitch, leaving openings at the top to insert a hanging rod and on one long side to turn. Press seams open, trim seam allowance in corners. Turn to right side. Slipstitch the opening on the side closed. Insert rod and hang.

Patterns on opposite page, from top to bottom: Design 2:6– Chidori; Koshi; Design 4:5–Nowaki

Sashiko Sheets and Pillowcases

Stitching sashiko on the hems of purchased sheets and pillowcases provides a wonderful opportunity to experiment with border designs. The designs used on the pillowcases here are kaki no hana (design 3:3), kaku shippo (design 3:19), inazuma (design 3:11), and selected lines from anasoha (design 5:3). The sheet uses kanmon (design 3:7).

MATERIALS + TOOLS

Purchased flat sheet and pair of pillowcases

Regular thread to match

One or two colors of contrasting topstitching-weight thread for sashiko

½ yard (.45 m) of 45" (1.14 m) white cotton fusible interfacing

Photocopies of sashiko designs

Iron-on transfer pens

INSTRUCTIONS

■ **1** ■ Remove the stitching from the top hem of the sheet and from the open ends of the pillowcases. Lightly press the hem area so that the sheet or pillowcase fabric lies flat but so you can still see the original hem fold line. (Note: If the hem of the sheet is not wide enough for the sashiko design of your choice, simply press a new hem and cut the interfacing to this width.)

■ **2** ■ Measure the depth of the hem from the fold line to the original stitching line and cut rows of the interfacing in this same width. (A queen-size sheet will take two 45" long rows of interfacing, while a standard-size pillow case will take only one 45"-long row of interfacing.)

■ **3** ■ Apply the interfacing to the wrong side of the body (not to the facing!) of the sheet or pillowcase in the area between the hem fold and the original hem's stitching line.

■ **4** ■ Cut your photocopies to the width of the interfacing, ink them, and let dry. Transfer the design from the photocopy to the interfacing. Stitch the sashiko design. Press the hem back in place and stitch to secure.

HELPFUL HINT

Find potential border designs in all over patterns by placing two pieces of plain white paper parallel to each other and laying them over full-scale sashiko designs. If a potential border pattern exists but the design is too large or to small, use a photocopier to reduce or enlarge the design until it fits within the border area. By stitching only some, rather than all the lines within the border, you can create entirely new patterns.

Coasters

A *single rectangle from the stitch dictionary makes three mini (3½", 9 cm square) coasters or two regular-sized ones (5", 13 cm square). These coasters began as nine thread samples on three rectangles to determine which threads to use for the vest on page 85. (Design 3:5 was used for all.)*

Designs 3:1 and 3:11 were used in these coasters so that you can get an idea of how different coasters made from the same rectangle can look. Several of the rectangles in the pattern dictionary have two designs on them. These are especially well-suited to making larger coasters because you will get two different looks from one rectangle.

MATERIALS + TOOLS

8½ x 11" (22 x 28 cm) rectangle of fashion fabric

8½ x 11" rectangle of white cotton fusible interfacing

Top-stitching-weight thread for sashiko

Regular sewing thread

Photocopies of sashiko patterns

Iron-on transfer pens

INSTRUCTIONS

■ **1** ■ Photocopy the desired sashiko pattern from the dictionary, ink with iron-on transfer pens, and let dry.

■ **2** ■ Apply the rectangle of fusible interfacing (glue side down) to the wrong side of the rectangle of fashion fabric according to manufacturer's directions.

■ **3** ■ Apply the sashiko design to the interfaced side of the rectangle and stitch. Cut rectangle as shown on the diagram below.

■ **4** ■ Referring to the diagram, fold each piece in half and stitch a ¼" (6 mm) seam on two sides. Measure the distance between these seams. Stitch the last seam this same distance from the first seam, leaving an opening in the middle to turn the coaster.

■ **5** ■ Trim the seam allowance on the last edge sewn, leaving a wide allowance in the open area. Trim the corners, then turn and press well. Slipstitch the opening closed.

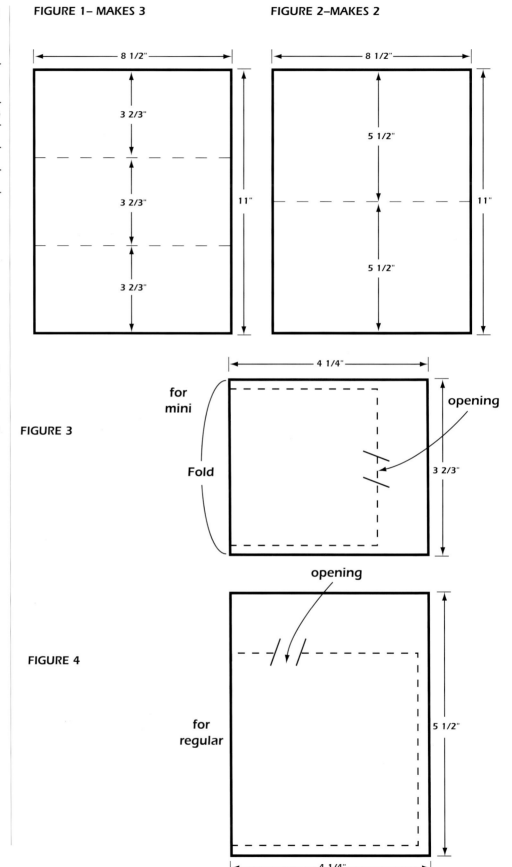

FIGURE 1– MAKES 3

FIGURE 2–MAKES 2

FIGURE 3

FIGURE 4

Sashiko Tote Bag

Any of the sashiko patterns shown in the book can be used to adorn the front of a tote bag. The example shown below uses the seigaiha (blue ocean waves) design, while the bag on page 61 uses the sakura (cherry blossom) design. Choose a lining fabric that echoes the sashiko design for an added touch.

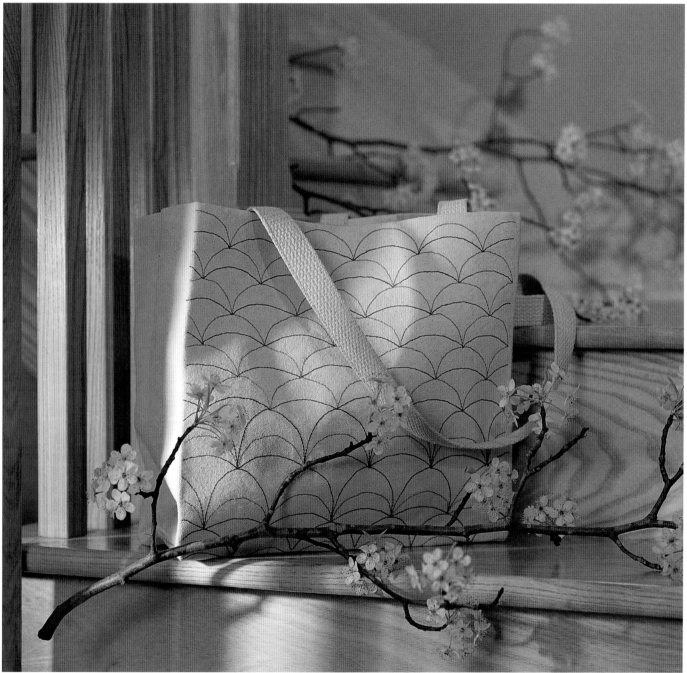

Design 4:1–Seigaiha

MATERIALS AND TOOLS

½ yard (.45 m) sturdy cotton fabric

½ yard printed cotton fabric for lining

⅜ yard (.38 m) white fusible cotton interfacing

3 yards (2.7 m) webbing for straps

Photocopy of chosen sashiko design

Iron-on transfer pens

Heavy thread for sashiko

Regular thread

INSTRUCTIONS

■ **1** ■ Trim the cotton fabric to 36¾ x 18" (93 x 46 cm). Cut a 12"-square (31 cm) piece of the white fusible cotton interfacing. Place the interfacing glue-side down on the wrong side of the tote fabric. Refer to Figure 1 for placement. Fuse the interfacing into place.

■ **2** ■ Mark a photocopy of your chosen sashiko design with iron-on transfer pens and let dry. Turn the marked photocopy face down on the cotton interfacing and transfer the design to the interfacing using transfer pens and following the manufacturer's instructions. Move the photocopy and overlap the design to cover the entire 12" area. Stitch the sashiko design.

■ **3** ■ Place your fabric on a flat surface. Cut three rectangles from the tote fabric as shown in Figure 2. Fold the fabric in half, right sides together, as shown in Figure 3. Stitch the side seam and the bottom seam in a ⅜" (9 mm) seam, leaving two unjoined areas at the bottom corners of the tote as shown in Figure 3. Insert both index fingers into one of these corners and pull the fabric taut so that the

unsewn portion from the bottom meets that from the side. Pin in place and sew a ⅜" seam. Repeat for the other corner.

■ **4** ■ With the tote still inside out, fold a 2½" (6.4 cm) "hem" of fabric at the top by turning the right side of the fabric to the outside. (The wrong sides of the tote fabric will be together inside this "hemmed" area.) Press, but don't sew.

■ **5** ■ Cut the webbing into two equal lengths. With the tote still inside out, shape one piece of webbing into a "U" and tuck each end into the seam allowance at the bottom of the tote, centering each piece of webbing 4" (10 cm) out from the center of the bottom of the tote. Make sure the same side is face up at both ends and don't twist the webbing. Stitch the ends of the webbing to the seam allowance.

■ **6** ■. Continue pinning the webbing against the wrong side of the tote fabric in parallel lines up to the edge of the hem at the top. Allow enough ease in the webbing so that it doesn't pull the tote fabric. When you reach the hem on each side, pin the webbing only to the hem, not through to the outer fabric. Release all of the pins except those holding the webbing to the hem, then repeat on the other side of the tote with the second piece of webbing. Stitch the webbing only to the hem area on both sides of the tote.

■ **7** ■ Cut the lining fabric as shown in Figure 2, but decrease the height from 18" to 13¾" (46 to 35 cm). With right sides together, start at the top and sew 3" (7.5 cm) of the side seam with a ⅜" seam. Press the seam open and turn the lining right side out.

Design 6:4–Sakvra

FIGURE 1

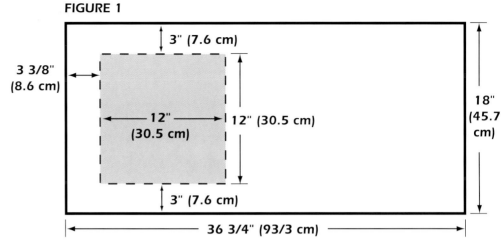

3" (7.6 cm)

3 3/8" (8.6 cm)

12" (30.5 cm)

12" (30.5 cm)

3" (7.6 cm)

18" (45.7 cm)

36 3/4" (93/3 cm)

FIGURE 2

Center of fabric

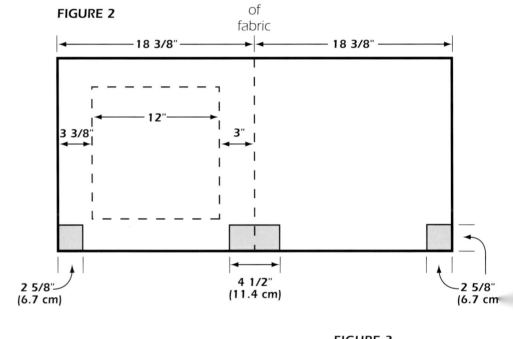

18 3/8"

18 3/8"

3 3/8"

12"

3"

2 5/8" (6.7 cm)

4 1/2" (11.4 cm)

2 5/8" (6.7 cm

■ **8** ■ With the right sides of the tote and lining together, match the side seams. Align the raw edges along the top of the tote and the lining and sew a ⅜" seam. Press the seam toward the lining.

■ **9** ■ Turn the lining, stitch 3" of the side seam from the bottom corner with right sides together. Press open. Pull the bottom of the lining through the unsewn middle area of the side seam and stitch the bottom seam with right sides together. Stitch the open corners as you did for the tote fabric in step 3.

■ **10** ■ Open the tote and stand it upright. Pin the lining and tote fabric together all along the rectangular base of the tote. Stitch the two fabrics together on your machine along this rectangular outline, removing the pins as you approach them to secure the handles of the tote and keep the lining from popping up. Slipstitch the opening in the side seam closed.

FIGURE 3

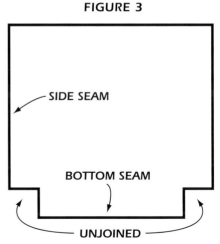

SIDE SEAM

BOTTOM SEAM

UNJOINED

Hexagonal Placemats

Clockwise from top center: design 6:3, Tsura; design 5:10—Mukai-Kikko; design 4:2—Seigaiha; design 4:10—Nashi; design 5:8—Bishamon; design 2:3—Shippo. Center: design 7:5—Koshi-Kuzushi

Many Japanese-inspired prints are available and it's fun to match linings to the designs used in the project. These placemats were designed to commemorate my mother's 90th birthday. The hexagonal shape echoes the tortoiseshell, which celebrates her longevity, while the sashiko designs convey wishes for her continued health and happiness. The tsuru (crane) and mukai-kikko (faced tortoiseshell) designs both symbolize long life. The seigaiha (blue ocean waves) pattern symbolizes eternity and immortality. The bishamon (Chinese god of wealth) pattern signifies prosperity, as does shippo (seven treasures of Buddha) through its association with precious metals and stones. The nashi (pear blossom) wishes wealth of another sort— the continued ability to appreciate the beauty of nature, while the koshi-kuzushi (letter "I") pattern in the middle tells my mother that she is still "number 1" (ichiban) to me.

MATERIALS + TOOLS

2 yards (1.8 m) of 45" (1.14 m) fashion fabric (makes six placemats)

2 yards of 45" lining fabric

2 yards of 45" white cotton fusible interfacing

Photocopies of chosen sashiko designs

Iron-on transfer pens

Heavy rayon thread for sashiko

Regular thread

PROJECT PLANNING

Measure the diameter of a circular table and divide by five. This number should be the finished measurement of each side of the hexagonal placemats. Create a pattern for your placemats by drawing a hexagon that has this measurement on each of its six sides. For example, for a 40"-diameter (1 m) table, the hexagon should be 8" (20.5 cm) on each side. Confirm your measurement by making six identical patterns from paper and laying them out on your table to make sure that they cover it. Add a seam allowance to each edge of one of the paper patterns and use it to cut out your fabric.

Mark the seven areas for the sashiko designs by drawing a second hexagon inside of your pattern so that a wide "border" forms all around its edge. Extend lines from the corners of the outer hexagon to the second, interior hexagon. Cut the pattern apart on these lines to make six rectangles. Cut your sashiko photocopies in the same size as these six rectangles and in the same size as the interior hexagon. Any seven designs can be used on the placemat, and the placemats can be designed in any size or shape you like.

INSTRUCTIONS

■ 1 ■ Cut the fabric, lining, and interfacing separately, using your custom hexagonal pattern. Apply the interfacing to the wrong side of the fabric.

■ 2 ■ Cut your sashiko photocopies to the appropriate size. Ink the photocopies and let them dry.

■ 3 ■ Transfer the designs to the interfacing and stitch the sashiko design.

■ 4 ■ Pin the lining and upper fabrics together with right sides together and stitch, leaving an opening along the longer straight side for turning.

■ 5 ■ Press seams open and trim seam allowance in corners. Turn to right side. Slipstitch the opening closed.

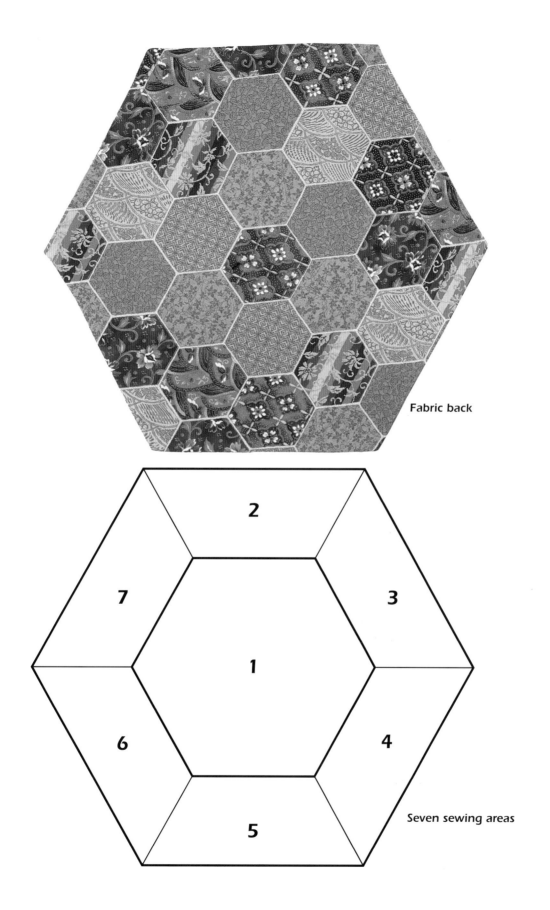

Fabric back

2

7   3

1

6   4

5

Seven sewing areas

Rectangular Placemats

When sewn together, two rectangles from the stitch dictionary make a great placemat. Finish the edges with purchased, extra-wide, double-fold bias tape or make your own binding as described here. The technique to apply the binding described here produces a folded miter finish. The pattern dictionary provides numerous examples of "companion" designs that join together well in a placemat. The placemats shown here are made from the following companion designs: designs 1:5 and 1:6 (plaids and checks); designs 2:6 and 2:7 (plovers and an interlaced circle of two birds); designs 3:7 and 3:8 (geometrics and thunderbolts); and designs 2:3 and 3:18 (seven treasures and angled seven treasures).

MATERIALS + TOOLS

*2 8½ x 11" (22 x 28 cm) rectangles of
fashion fabric (per placemat)*

*Strip of fashion fabric 11" long x 2"
wide, cut on straight of grain, for
joining*

*Strip of fashion fabric 60" long x 3¼"
wide, cut on straight of grain, for
binding*

*17 x 11" rectangle of printed cotton
for bottom of placemat (one yard will
make six)*

*50 mm (2" wide) bias tape maker
(optional, but very helpful)*

*2 8½ x 11" rectangles of white cotton
fusible interfacing*

Top-stitching-weight thread for sashiko

Regular sewing thread

Photocopies of sashiko patterns

Iron-on transfer pens

INSTRUCTIONS

■ **1** ■ Ink the sashiko photocopies
with iron-on transfer pens and let dry.
Apply the rectangle of fusible interfacing (glue side down) to the wrong
side of the fashion fabric according to
manufacturer's directions. Apply the
sashiko design to the interfaced side
of the rectangles and stitch.

■ **2** ■ Abut the two rectangles
together, face up, as you want them to
appear when they are permanently
stitched together. Lay the 11 x 2"
strip right side down against the 11"
center side of one of the rectangles,
matching raw edges. Pin and stitch.
Press seam toward piecing strip.

■ **3** ■ Place the rectangle back on
the table in its original position, then
flip it over on top of the other rectangle so that the other 11" raw edge of
the piecing strip is now even with the

center 11" raw edge. Pin and stitch.
Press seam toward piecing strip.

■ **4** ■ If you have a 50 mm (2" wide)
bias tape maker, use it to turn ⅝" (15
mm) under on each long edge of the
60" strip to form a 2"-wide strip. If
you don't have a bias tape maker,
press up a ⅝" "hem" on each long
side of the 60" strip, then fold the
strip in half lengthwise, favoring the
bottom edge so that it extends ⅛" (3
mm) beyond the top edge.

■ **5** ■ Layer your placemat together
with the lining right side down and
the sashiko rectangles right side up on
top. Baste around all edges of the rectangle. Open up the tape and fold back
½" (13 mm) across one short end.
Place that end even with the seam line
at the center bottom of the placemat
with right sides together and raw edges
even. The line that was formed when
one side of the strip was pressed under
⅝" should now be on the ⅝" stitching
line for the placemat.

■ **6** ■ Sew on that line, stopping ⅝"
from the corner of the rectangle, and
backstitch to secure stitching. Lift up
the strip and refold against the rectangle so that the area you just sewed
is folded back against itself, forming a
triangle. Square-off the top of the
strip against the corner of the placemat. Resume stitching ⅝" out from
the corner on the ⅝" pressed hem
line and continue until you are within
⅝" of the next corner.

■ **7** ■ Repeat step 6 for each edge of
the placemat until you are back at
your initial starting point. Overlap the
edge of the binding by ½" and trim
off excess binding.

■ **8** ■ Turn the binding right side
out, folding it around the edge of the
placemat. Pin in place on the top side
in the "ditch" between the binding
and the placemat, making sure that
the binding on the underside extends
far enough to be caught when you
"stitch in the ditch" from the top
side. Stitch in the ditch.

Small Wall Hanging

The sashiko patterns used in this wall hanging illustrate both how several designs can be formed from the same design line and how sashiko patterns build on each other. The same curved design line builds either the amime (fishing net) pattern or the chidori (plover) pattern. These combine to form toridasuki (interconnected circle of two birds). When an additional semicircular embellishment is added, the design ultimately forms hanmaru, a pattern of interconnected semicircles. Any of the designs shown in this book could be substituted for the nine patterns chosen for the nine quilt blocks.

MATERIALS + TOOLS

1¼ yards (1.13 m) of 40" (1 m) or wider fashion fabric for quilt front

1⅛ yards (1 m) of 36" (.9 m) or wider fashion fabric for quilt back

4½ yards (4.05 m) quilt binding (or enough fabric to make your own wide bias binding)

Six different colors of top-stitching weight thread

Regular sewing thread

1 yard (.9 m) white cotton fusible interfacing

Iron-on transfer pens

INSTRUCTIONS

■ **1** ■ Cut the quilt front fabric into the following pieces, following the cutting layout: nine rectangles measuring 8½" wide x 11" long (21.5 x 28 cm); six strips measuring 2" wide x 9" long (5 x 23 cm); two strips measuring 2" wide x 33" long (5 x 84 cm); two strips measuring 3¼" wide x 32" long (8.25 x 81 cm); two strips measuring 3¼" wide x 39" long (8.25 x 99 cm).

■ **2** ■ Cut nine 8½ x 11" rectangles of white cotton fusible interfacing and fuse them to the wrong side of the fashion fabric rectangles according to manufacturer's directions. Ink photocopies of both version A and B of hanmaru with iron-on transfer pens and let dry.

■ **3** ■ Place an old pressing cloth on your ironing board to absorb any color that may bleed. (Some of the color may "bleed" off the transfer.) Transfer the color-coded stitching patterns from one of the *hanmaru* designs shown at the right to the interfaced side of a rectangle. Continue until you have made three transfers from version A

(these will be used for the top row) and three from version B (these will be used for the bottom row). Mark the three remaining transfers on the rectangles from either version A or version B.

■ **4** ■ Stitch the color coded lines on the nine rectangles. Arrange the stitched rectangles on a table in the sequence shown on the diagram. Abut the rectangles in each column so that their horizontal edges are touching. Lay one of the 2"-wide x 9"-long strips along the top of each rectangle that has another rectangle above it, placing right sides together, and pin into place. Stitch together in a ½" (13 mm) seam.

■ **5** ■ Place the sewn rectangles and strips back on the table. Flip each rectangle over so that its edge is even with the bottom of the rectangle that was above it and so that right sides are together. Pin in place and sew in a ½" seam. Continue this process of sewing strips to the top and bottom of each rectangle until all six 9" strips have been sewn to rectangles and the entire set of rectangles is now connected into columns.

■ **6** ■ Recheck the blocks to make sure that they are in the same sequence shown on the diagram. Lay one of the 2"-wide x 33"-long strips along the right side of the left column of rectangles with right sides facing. Pin into place and stitch together in a ½" seam. Press the seam toward the piecing strip.

■ **7** ■ Lay the column back on the table and flip it over so that the raw edge of the 33" long strip is aligned with the left side of the middle col-

umn of rectangles, right sides facing. Pin into place and stitch together in a ½" seam. Press the seam toward the piecing strip.

■ **8** ■ Place the other 2" wide by 33" long strip along the right side of the middle column of rectangles with right sides facing. Pin into place and stitch together in a ½" seam. Press seam toward the piecing strip.

■ **9** ■ Place the sewn column and strips back on the table. Flip the left column/strips piece over so that its right edge is even with the right edge of the left column of rectangles and so that right sides of both fabrics are together. Pin in place and sew in a ½" seam. Press the seam toward the piecing strip.

■ **10** ■ Center the 3¼" x 39" strips on the vertical edges of the quilt's top with right sides facing so that the strips extend approximately 2¾" beyond the quilt top at both the upper and lower edges. Sew to the quilt body with a ½" seam, stopping your stitching ½" from the upper and lower edges of the quilt top. Press the seam open.

■ **11** ■ Center the 3¼ x 32" strips on the horizontal edges of the quilt top with right sides facing so that the strips extend approximately 2¾" beyond the quilt's top at both the left and right edges. Sew to the quilt body with a ½" seam, stopping your stitching ½" from the left and right edges of the quilt top. Press the seam open.

■ **12** ■ Sew the strips together, mitering the corners. Press the seam open. Place the lining and pieced quilt on top of each other with wrong sides facing. Trim the lining to the dimensions

of the wall hanging. Pin in place through both layers. Stitch ⅛" (3 mm) outside each rectangle to secure the layers together. Stitch ½" from the edge all around the wall hanging.

■ **13** ■ Finish the wall hanging with bias quilt binding (or make your own binding from the same fabric used for the lining). Hand sew purchased hanging loops on the back of the wall hanging. Finished size: 31 x 38.5" (79 x 98 cm).

Cutting Layout

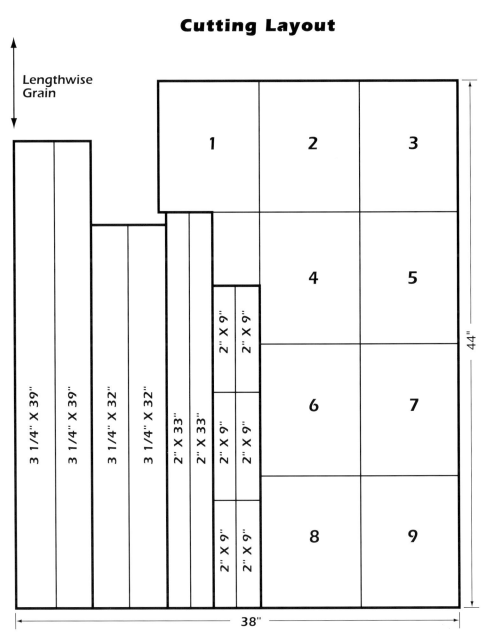

Lengthwise Grain

1   2   3

4   5

6   7

8   9

3 1/4" X 39"

3 1/4" X 39"

3 1/4" X 32"

3 1/4" X 32"

2" X 33"

2" X 33"

2" X 9"

2" X 9"

2" X 9"

2" X 9"

2" X 9"

2" X 9"

44"

38"

Wall Hanging Diagram

Sew only blue yellow, red and green lines of version A of the Interconnected Semi-circles pattern	Sew only red and green lines of version A of the Interconnected Semi-circles pattern	Sew only blue and yellow lines of version A of the Interconnected Semi-circles pattern
Sew only the pink and purple lines of either version of the Interconnected Semi-circles pattern	Sew all lines of the Interconnected Semi-circles pattern (either version)	Sew only the pink and purple lines of either versionn of the Interconnected Semi-circles pattern
Sew onlyblue and yellow lines of version B of the Interconnected Semicircles pattern	Sew only red and green lines of version B of the Interconnected Semicircles pattern	Sew only blue, yellow, red, and green lines of version B of the Interconnected Semi-circles pattern

Version A

Version B

Crib Quilt

The sashiko patterns used in the crib quilt convey specific wishes for the newborn: Long life from the tortoiseshell pattern, kasane kikko; a happy childhood from the toy building block pattern, tsumiki; success and power from the three scales pattern, uroko; and a sturdy body and rapid growth from the hemp leaf pattern, asanoha. The brightly colored stitching is part of the quilt's appeal, but it also allows the interrelationship between the four designs to be seen easily. Thus the quilt makes another wish: that the child's artistic ability awakes early in life. (See the full quilt on page 18.)

Version A

Version B

HELPFUL HINT

Find potential border designs in all over patterns by placing two pieces of plain white paper parallel to each other and laying them over full-scale sashiko designs.

MATERIALS + TOOLS

1½ yards (1.35 m) of fashion fabric 45" (1.14 m) or wider for quilt front

1⅜ yards (1.24 m) of fashion fabric 36" (91 cm) or wider for quilt back

1⅜ yards 36" or wider batting

4½ (4 m) yards quilt binding (or enough fabric to make your own wide bias binding)

7 different colors of top-stitching-weight thread

Regular sewing thread to match quilt front fabric

2 yards (1.8 m) of iron-on, temporary-fuse paper stabilizer 20" (51 cm) wide

Teflon pressing sheet

Iron-on transfer pens

INSTRUCTIONS

■ **1** ■ Cut the quilt front fabric into the following pieces, following the cutting layout shown at the right: nine rectangles 8½" wide x 11" long (22 x 11 cm); two strips 2" wide x 35" long (5 x 89 cm); four strips 2" wide x 25½" long (5 x 65 cm); two strips 4" wide x 25½" long (10 x 65 cm); two strips 3¼" wide x 31" long (8.25 x 79 cm); two strips 3¼" wide x 44½" long (8.25 x 113 cm).

■ **2** ■ Cut nine 8½" x11" rectangles and two strips measuring 4" wide x 25½" long of white iron-on stabilizer.

■ **3** ■ Place the teflon pressing sheet on your ironing board and lay one rectangle of the white iron-on removable paper stabilizer, shiny side down, on top of the sheet. Use the stabilizer manufacturer's recommended iron temperature to transfer the color-coded stitching patterns from one of the *asanoha* designs to the dull side of the stabilizer rectangle. After the

color transfer is complete, remove the stabilizer rectangle from the teflon sheet and set aside. Continue until you have made three transfers from version A (these will be used for the bottom row) and three from version B (these will be used for the top row). The three remaining transfers on the rectangles may be from either version A or version B. Also make two transfers on the strips of the asanoha border design.

■ **4** ■ Replace the teflon pressing sheet with an old pressing cloth. Place a rectangle of quilt fabric, right side down, on the ironing board, then place a rectangle of stabilizer, shiny side down, on top of the quilt fabric. The color coding on the stabilizer should be facing up.

■ **5** ■ Using your iron, lightly tack the stabilizer to the quilt fabric. Some of the color may "bleed" off the transfer as you iron on to the surrounding press cloth fabric, but not enough to interfere with your stitching. (Be sure to use a pressing cloth or your ironing board cover will absorb the color.) Repeat this process for both 4"-wide by 25½"-long fabric strips.

■ **6** ■ Stitch the color coded lines on the nine rectangles and the two strips. Tear away the temporary stabilizer. Arrange the rectangles on a table in the sequence shown on the diagram. Abut the rectangles in each row so that their lengthwise edges are touching. Lay one of the 2"-wide x 25½"-long strips along the top of the upper row of rectangles, right side together, and pin into place. Stitch together in a ½" seam. Lay another of the 2"-wide x 25½"-long strips along the bottom of the upper row of

Cutting Layout

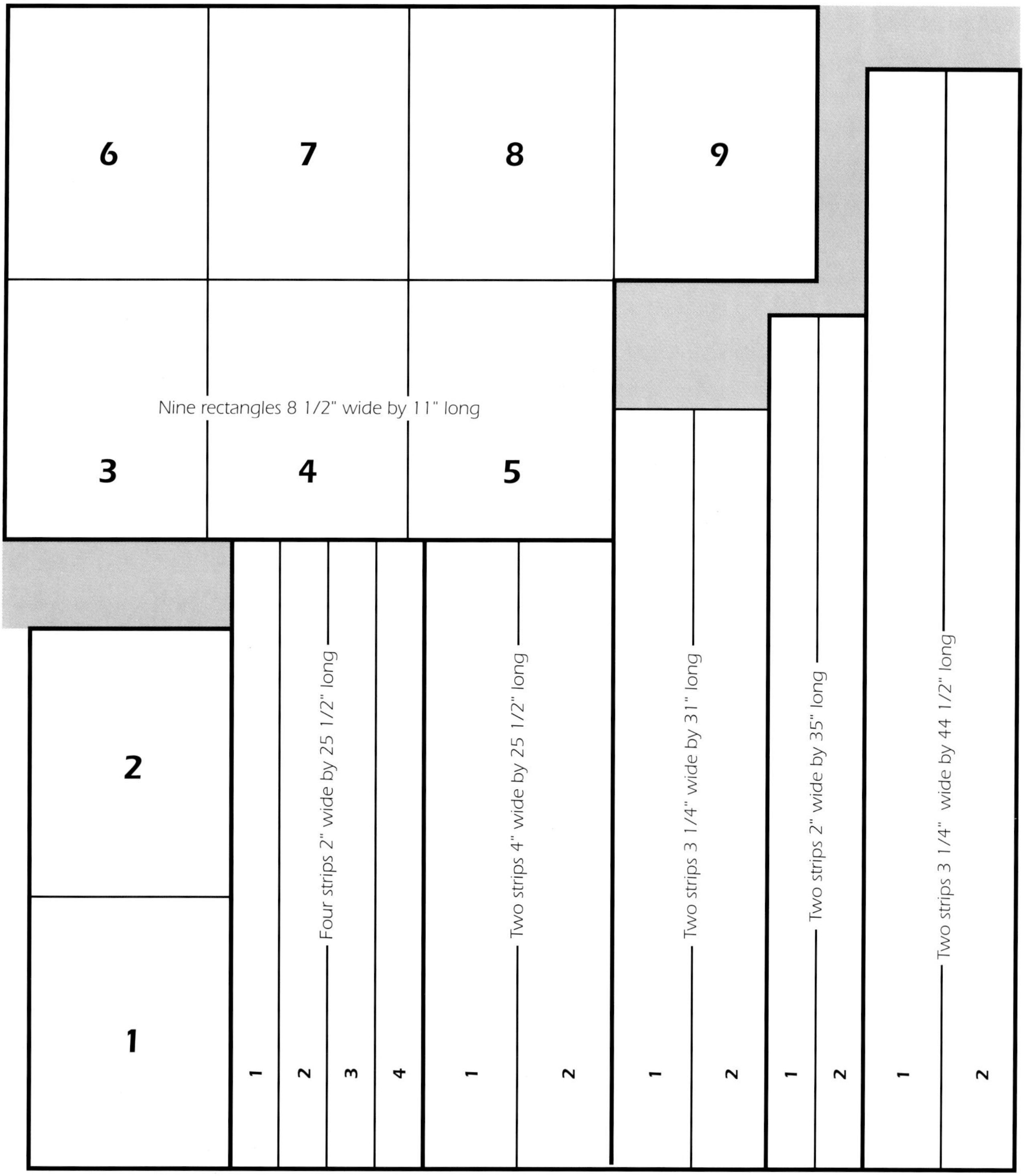

Nine rectangles 8 1/2" wide by 11" long

6	7	8	9
3	4	5	

2

1

Four strips 2" wide by 25 1/2" long

1
2
3
4

Two strips 4" wide by 25 1/2" long

1
2

Two strips 3 1/4" wide by 31" long

1
2

Two strips 2" wide by 35" long

1
2

Two strips 3 1/4" wide by 44 1/2" long

1
2

Hemp Leaf Insert		
Sew only blue, yellow, red, and green lines of version A of the hemp leaf pattern	Sew only red and green lines of version A of the hemp leaf pattern	Sew only blue and yellow lines of version A of the hemp leaf pattern
Sew only pink, purple, and orange lines of either version of the hemp leaf pattern	Sew all lines of the hemp leaf pattern (either version)	Sew only pink, purple, and orange lines of either version of the hemp leaf pattern
Sew only blue and yellow lines of version B of the hemp leaf pattern	Sew only red and green lines of version B of the hemp leaf pattern	Sew only blue, yellow, red, and green lines of version B of the hemp leaf pattern
Hemp Leaf Insert		

rectangles, right sides together, and pin into place. Stitch together in a ½" seam.

■ **7** ■ Place the sewn rectangles and strips back on the table. Flip the bottom strip over so that its edge is even with the top of the middle row of rectangles and so that right sides are together. Pin in place and sew in a ½" seam. Continue this process of sewing strips to the top and bottom of each row of rectangles until all four strips have been sewn to rectangles and the entire set of rectangles is connected by strips.

■ **8** ■ Cut the strips apart between the rectangles so that three long columns of rectangles result. Lay the columns back on the table, making sure that the blocks are in the same sequence shown on the diagram. Lay one of the 2"-wide x 35"-long strips along the left side of the left column of rectangles, right side of the fabric together, and pin into place. Stitch together in a ½" seam. Lay another of the 2"-wide x 35"-long strips along the right side of the left column of rectangles, right sides of the fabric together, and pin into place. Stitch together in a ½" seam.

■ **9** ■ Place the sewn column and strips back on the table. Flip the left column/strips piece over so that its right edge is even with the left edge of the middle row of rectangles and so that right sides of both pieces of fabric are together. Pin in place and sew in a ½" seam. Continue this process of sewing strips to the right and left of each row of rectangles until all four strips have been sewn to rectangles and the entire set of rectangles is connected by the strips. Sew the 4" x 25½" inserts to the top and bottom of the quilt top.

■ **10** ■ Center the longer (3¼" x 44½") plain strips of fashion fabric on the vertical edges of the quilt top, with right sides of the fabrics together so that the strips extend approximately 2½" beyond the quilt top at both upper and lower edges. Sew to the quilt body with a ½" seam, stopping your stitching ½" from the upper and lower edges of the quilt top. Press the seam open.

■ **11** ■ Center the shorter (3¼" x 31") plain strips of fashion fabric on the horizontal edges of the quilt top, with right sides of the fabrics together so that the strips extend approximately 2½" beyond the quilt top at both left and right edges. Sew to the quilt body with a ½" seam, stopping your stitching ½" from the left and right edges of the quilt top. Press the seam open. Sew the strips together, mitering the corners. Press the seams open.

■ **12** ■ Layer the batting between the quilt back fabric and the quilt top with right sides facing out. Pin in place through all layers. Trim the batting and quilt back fabric to match the finished dimensions of the quilt top. Stitch ⅛" (3 mm) outside each rectangle to secure the three layers together. Finish the quilt with bias quilt binding. Finished dimensions: 30 x 45" long (.76 x 1.14 m).

Sashiko Screen Panels

These screen panels create a stunning room display and can be made from any 20 of the designs shown in the pattern dictionary. A single panel can be used as a wall hanging.

MATERIALS + TOOLS

1⅞ yards (1.69 m) of 60" (1.52 m) wide fabric for front of hanging

1¾ yards (1.58 m) of 45" (1.14 m) or wider fabric for lining

1¼ yards (1.12 m) of 45" white cotton fusible interfacing

5 pieces of mending tape, each measuring 10" (2.5 cm) long by ½" (13 mm) wide pieces of iron-on mending tape

3–4 spools of top-stitching weight thread

Regular sewing thread

20 photocopies of sashiko designs

Iron-on transfer pens

INSTRUCTIONS

■ 1 ■ On the lengthwise grain of the fabric, cut five strips measuring 2" wide x 65" long (5 cm x 1.65 m); cut six strips measuring 2" wide x 34" long (5 x 86 cm); and cut 20 rectangles measuring 8½ by 11" from the fashion fabric and the interfacing. (You can cut the interfacing rectangles four rows of five across with the 11" edge on the lengthwise grain.) Refer to Figure 1 for cutting layout.

■ 2 ■ Place a rectangle of interfacing glue-side down on the wrong side of a rectangle of fabric and fuse in place according to manufacturer's directions. Repeat for the other 19 rectangles.

■ 3 ■ Mark the 20 photocopies with iron-on transfer pens, let dry, and iron onto the interfacing side of the rectangles. Sew the sashiko designs on each of the 20 rectangles. Lay out all of the sewn rectangles to determine how you want them to be placed

in the finished wall hanging.

■ 4 ■ To sew the bottom row of the wall hanging together, place the four rectangles that will be in that row together face up on a table so that they are abutting each other along their 11" sides to form a 34"-wide row.

■ 5 ■ Pin one of the 34" strips in place face down on the lower edge of the rectangles. Sew together in a ½" (13 mm) seam, and press the seam so that the rectangles are flat rather than turned back on themselves.

■ 6 ■ Return the rectangles and the strip to the table so that the rectangles are again face up and the sewn strip is at the bottom. Pin a second 34" strip in place face down on the upper edge of the rectangles. Sew a ½" seam and press the seam as directed above.

■ 7 ■ Lay the second row of rectangles face up on the table so that they are abutting each other along their 11" sides. Flip the part of the hanging that you have already sewn together so that you are placing the raw edge of the upper sewn strip right side down on the lower edge of the four new rectangles. Pin and sew a ½" seam. Press as directed above.

■ 8 ■ Return your work to the table so that the rectangles face up and the bottom row is at the bottom. Pin a third 34" strip in place face down on the upper edge of this row of rectangles. Sew a ½" seam. Press.

■ 9 ■ Repeat these steps until you have sewn together all five rows and used all six 34" strips. All the rectangles will be joined along their tops and bottoms when you have finished

and their 11" sides will still be unsewn.

■ 10 ■ Cut the 34" strips apart between the rectangles so that you have four 55"-long joined strips of 8½"-wide rectangles. Place the left-most strip of rectangles face up on a table. Pin one of the 65"-long strips right side down on the left side of the strip of rectangles, having the bottom edge of the 65" strip even with the bottom edge of the rectangles. (The extra 10" at the top will be used to make a hanging loop for the wall hanging.) Sew in a ½" seam, stopping ½" short of the top of the hanging. Press the seam so that the rectangles are flat rather than turned back on themselves.

■ 11 ■ Lay the strip of rectangles back down on the table, and pin a second 65"-long strip right side down along its right side, having the bottom edge of the 65" strip even with the bottom edge of the strip of rectangles. Pin and sew a ½" seam, stopping ½" short of the top of the hanging. Press the seam so that the rectangles are flat rather than turned back on themselves.

■ 12 ■ Lay your second leftmost strip of rectangles face up on the table. Flip the part of the wall hanging that you have already sewn so that you are placing the raw edge of the strip that has been sewn to first strip of rectangles right side down on the left edge of the second strip of rectangles. Pin and sew a ½" seam, stopping ½" short of the top of the hanging. Press the seam so that the rectangles are flat rather than turned back on themselves.

■ 13 ■ Return your work to the table

so that the rectangles face up and the newly sewn strip is in the middle of the two strips of rectangles. Be sure that your left-most row is at the far left. Pin a third 65" strip in place face down on the right edge of the right row of rectangles, having the bottom edge of the 65" strip even with the bottom edge of the strip of rectangles. Sew a $\frac{1}{2}$" seam, stopping $\frac{1}{2}$" short of the top of the hanging. Press the seam so that the rectangles are flat rather than turned back on themselves.

■ **14** ■ Repeat these steps until all five 65" strips are sewn between all four strips of rectangles and on both outside edges. Press under $\frac{1}{2}$" along the edge of each side of the 10" extensions at the top of the hanging. Apply iron-on tape to the underside of the extensions to secure the pressed-under edges and to reinforce the fabric that will become the hanging loops.

■ **15** ■ Lay the backing fabric right side up on the table, then lay the hanging right side down on top of it and pin the two together along the sides and the bottom. Stitch together in a $\frac{1}{2}$" seam along the sides and bottom. Trim off any excess backing fabric, turn the hanging right side out, and press. Press under $\frac{1}{2}$" on the upper edge of the hanging and $\frac{1}{2}$" on the upper edge of the backing. Pin the extensions between the hanging and the backing such that loops are formed. Pin the rest of the hanging and lining top edges together. Top-stitch the top edge closed.

Cutting Layout

Each square is 8½" x 11"

17	18	19	20
13	14	15	16
9	10	11	12
5	6	7	8
1	2	3	4

1 2 3 4 5

1 2 3 4 5 6

65"

34"

Sashiko Fashion

Because of the vast array of fabrics, threads and clothing patterns available, wearables provide the ultimate "canvas" for self-expression and creativity. Although sashiko stitching was originally used on clothing for an entirely practical purpose—to quilt layers of fabric together for warmth—the techniques in the book allow you to turn sashiko designs into an ethereal embellishment. The photographs in this section are intended to inspire your own creative efforts. The clothing shown represents not only my own work, but also that of two of my longtime friends and professional colleagues whom I introduced to sashiko several years ago. All three of us enjoy our coworkers' delight each time we wear one of our creations at work. We all find that wearing creatively stitched clothing seems to make us more creative in our day-to-day jobs.

A temporary stabilizer allows you to stitch sashiko on fabrics as lightweight, delicate, and transparent as silk chiffon. The concept for this garment and the one on page 85 resulted from discussions with the staff of Threads magazine. The sashiko design on the garment was adapted from the traditional seigaiha pattern. Both first appeared in issue #82. The look of subtle elegance is achieved by stitching the sashiko with a shiny rayon serger-weight thread in a color very close to that of the silk chiffon itself.

■ This top and the one on page 86 show how fabric and embellishment choices can make garments so unique that they seem to "owe" nothing to each other, even when the same fashion pattern is used. This garment used three drapey rayon solids and embellished the upper back area with the variant of the kiku design shown in the upper left-hand corner of design 6:7.

Designer: Anne Davidson

■ The sashiko is stitched with pearl cotton (size # 5) in colors that provide a high contrast to the linen background. Because the vest is completely lined, a permanent interfacing can carry the color-coded stitching lines. The stitching combines tachibana (design 6:9) with untitled Hokusai #3 (design 3:5). Both the fabric and thread choices and the embellishment concept for this vest were developed by the art department staff of Threads magazine.

Even if you don't have time to sew a complete garment, you can still apply sashiko embellishment to purchased clothing. For example, you can carefully remove a pocket from a purchased blouse, apply temporary iron-on paper stabilizer to its wrong size to carry your stitching pattern, remove the stabilizer after stitching is complete, and then simply reattach the pocket. The kiku pattern is in the center of design 6:7.

Designer:
Mary Parker

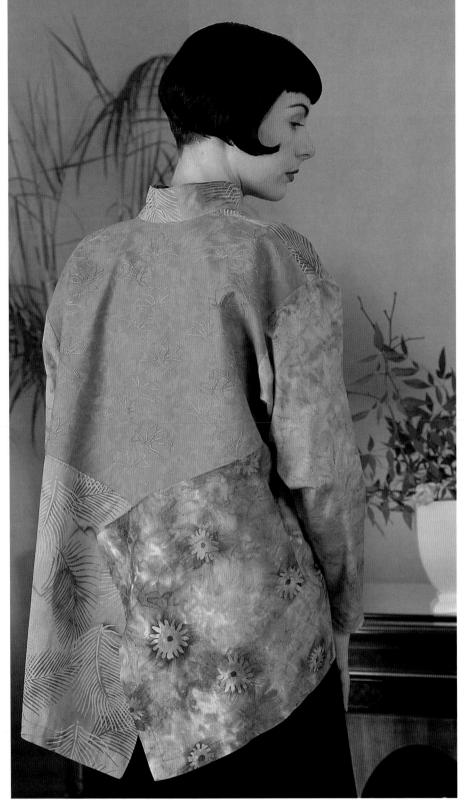

■ Printed and dyed cotton fabrics in complementary styles highlight the individually sewn tsuru patterns (design 6:3) on the solid upper back panel. Regular top-stitching-weight thread was used for the sashiko stitching.

Designer: Pat Thomas

■ This jacket is distinguished by its innovative combination of solid silk fabric (upon which the sashiko is stitched) with cottons printed in similar patterns. The sashiko on the long front panel is the matsukawa-bishi pattern (design 2:5). The serger-weight rayon thread used for the sashiko stitching complements the silk background fabric.

Designer: Pat Thomas

CHAPTER 4 Pattern Dictionary

The patterns in this dictionary will provide you with years of inspiration. They have beem divided into eight groups to help you develop your sashiko sewing skills in a systematic way. You should master the techniques required in one group before attempting patterns in the next group. (The first number in the design code shows the group to which a pattern belongs.) The groups are described below.

Group 1: *Designs formed with continuous straight lines.*

Group 2: *Designs formed with continuous curves.*

Group 3: *Designs formed by straight lines with pivots*

Group 4: *Designs formed by curves with pivots*

Group 5: *Designs formed by straight lines with pivots and double stitching*

Group 6: *Designs formed by curves with pivots and double stitching*

Group 7: *Traditional broken stitch patterns*

Group 8: *Motifs from crest designs*

The patterns have also been sequenced within each group so you can see how easily you can vary a basic design by substituting multiple lines for single lines, changing the amount of

space between sewn lines, or rotating and miror-imaging design lines. The more easily sewn patterns within each group are always presented first, with patterns increasing in complexity as more lines are used, curves are tighter, or line segment length is reduced.

Grouping together patterns that use the same design line (the design line is always shown in black) will also help you develop your own original, continuously stitched project designs. For example, you could stitch a rectangular wall hanging that started with *amime* (design 2:5), eased into *toridasuki* (design 2:7), and ended with *chidori* (design 2:6). The hanging could symbolize the transition of the seasons from summer to fall.

SEWING REMINDERS

Before sewing the designs that involve pivots or double stitching, you will need to practice calibrating your stitch length to the shortest line segment in a design. This technique is covered on pages 16-17. Many of the techniques discussed in that section also facilitate sewing traditional broken stitch patterns and crest designs.

To prevent pulling the fabric off grain as you stitch, sew vertical lines first, sew horizontal lines next, and diagonal lines last. Vertical lines should be sewn on the lengthwise grain of the fabric and horizontal lines should be sewn on the cross-grain of the fabric.

The relatively tight curves in some designs may be extremely challenging to sew on a machine that does not include a "needle down" feature. If your machine does not have "needle down," you may wish to enlarge the designs on a photocopier to make the curves easier to sew.

You can easily personalize designs by adding

additional stitching lines parallel to the basic design line. A quilting foot can be used as a guide to sew a precise ¼" (6mm) distance from the original lines of the design. Such stitching is shown in red on samples in this pattern dictionary. (The drawn pattern is shown in white thread.)

PERIODS OF JAPANESE HISTORY

In the commentary in the pattern dictionary, the historical origins of a design are given when they are known. The following periods of Japanese history are often mentioned. To conserve space, only the name of the period is given, not its time span. The table below shows the dates of each period of Japanese history.

Jomon ca. 8,000 B.C. to 300 B.C.

Yayoi ca. 300 B.C. to 300 A.D.

Tumulus ca. 300 A.D. to 552 A.D.

Asuka 552 A.D. to 710 A.D.

Nara 710 A.D. to 794 A.D.

Heian 794 A.D. to 1185 A.D.

Kamakura 1185 A.D. to 1336 A.D.

Muromachi 1336 A.D. to 1568 A.D.

Azuchi-Momoyama 1568 A.D. to 1603 A.D.

Tokugawa (Edo) 1603 A.D. to 1868 A.D.

Meiji 1868 A. D. to 1912 A.D.

Taisho 1912 A.D. to 1926 A.D.

Showa 1926 A.D. to 1989 A.D.

Heisei 1989 A.D. to Present

KATSUSHIKA HOKUSAI

In the narrative, the artist Katsushika Hokusai (1760 – 1849) is also frequently mentioned. One of his books, *Shingata Komoncho* (*New Forms for Design*) published in 1824, apparently served as the inspiration for many sashiko designs still in use today.

Katsushika Hokusai, self portrait

VERTICAL STRIPES

Patterns made by sewing parallel straight lines, or stripes, can be found on many antique sashiko-stitched garments in Japanese museums. A particularly interesting tradition developed on the island of Sado in the Sea of Japan. There, women divers sewed lines of sashiko stitching very closely together to create thick vertical stripes on their jackets. The best divers wore the thickest stripes.

The upper classes did not wear stripes until the Muromachi and Azuchi-Momoyama periods. Silks with colorful woven stripes were first imported into Japan at that time, and Japanese silk-producing facilities in Kyoto emulated them. Such fabrics were used in costumes for the Noh theater. Later, during the Meiji period, vertical stripes were also used extensively for costumes for the Kabuki theater. The use of striped costumes in both popular theaters increased their use throughout Japanese society. Vertical stripes were frequently used because they emphasized the design lines of the traditional kimono.

VERTICAL STRIPES

Vertically striped patterns (designs 1:1 and 1:2) are called *tate-jima*. *Tate-jima* designs are ideal for filling large areas between other designs in a quilt or wall hanging. *Tate-jima's* simplicity creates a visual counterpoint to complex or curved sashiko patterns in both home fashions and clothing.

DESIGN 1:1
Tate-Jima
VERTICAL STRIPES

竪縞

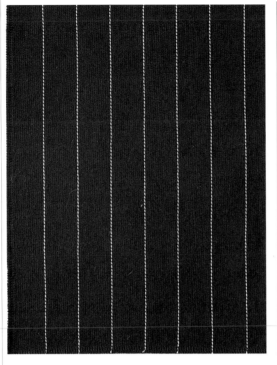

DESIGN 1:2
Tate-Jima
VERTICAL STRIPES

竪縞

DESIGN 1:3
Yoko-Jima
HORIZONTAL STRIPES

横縞

Because variations in fiber dyes often made unintended stripes in peasants' woven clothing, the Japanese continued for centuries to associate any striped pattern with the lower classes and casual clothing.

Horizontal stripes (designs 1:3 and 1:4) are called *yoko-jima*. Among commoners horizontal stripes were more popular than vertical stripes. Paintings from the Heian period show that clothing was decorated with various kinds of evenly placed horizontal striped designs. Many antique sashiko-stitched garments have evenly spaced horizontal stitching on the body and sleeves of the garment, complementing more intricate designs in the shoulder/yoke area. Modern Japanese sashiko pieces use irregularly spaced vertical or horizontal lines to cover large areas.

DESIGN 1:4
Yoko-Jima
HORIZONTAL STRIPES

横縞

HORIZONTAL STRIPES

The triple-line pattern shown in design 1:4 is the basis for other sashiko designs. The version of *yabane* shown in design 7:1, for example, uses this same line spacing, but breaks the stitching to leave intervals of unsewn space in the horizontal line as an additional design element.

91

CHECKS

Tate-jima and *yoko-jima* patterns can be combined (like designs 1:5 and 1:6) to make checks or plaids that are called *koshi*. These designs are not always sewn on the vertical/horizontal axes, but always use right angles. Textiles decorated with *koshi* patterns became popular during the Meiji period when they were used extensively for Kabuki theater costumes.

Many traditional sashiko patterns use the *koshi* grid. Stopping and starting the stitching at various points on the horizontal and/or vertical axis creates different designs. For example, see the *hirai-jumon* and *koshi gasuri* patterns (design 7:2). Comparing those two designs with the *koshi* grid reveals a fundamental principle of Japanese design: the unstitched areas are as significant to total design as the stitched areas.

PLAID WORN BY NAKAMURA FAMILY

In design 1:6, only half of the lines in the basic grid are stitched. An additional line (stitched in red) has been inserted between them to form a triplet. This plaid is as easy to sew as design 1:5, but it looks more sophisticated. The Nakamuras, a family of famous Kabuki actors, used this design for their signature "riddle" plaid. Ideographs for "*naka*" and "*ra*" were inserted into some of the large squares to suggest their family name. Their fans wore similar plaids to theater productions.

DESIGN 1:5
Koshi
CHECKS

格子

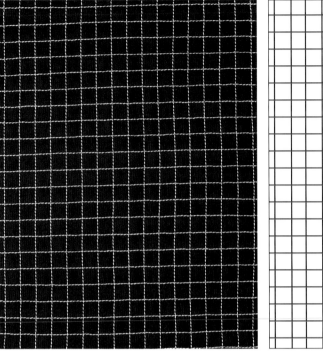

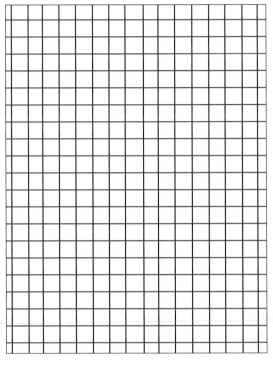

DESIGN 1:6
Nakamura Koshi
PLAID WORN BY NAKAMURA FAMILY

中村格子

DESIGN 1:7
Koshi
OVERLAID CHECK PATTERN

格子

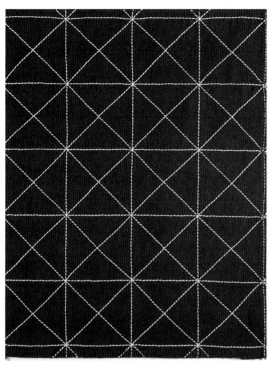

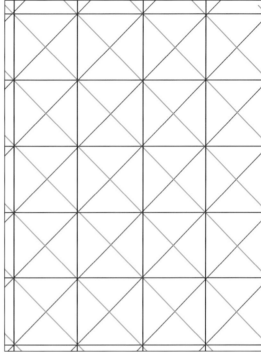

DESIGN 1:8
Hishi-moyo
DIAMONDS

菱模様

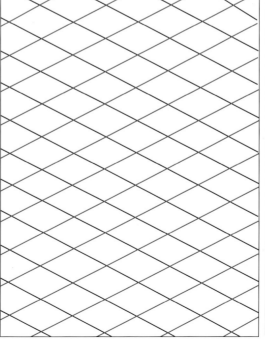

OVERLAID CHECK PATTERN

In the Edo period, a design made by overlaying two *koshi* patterns became popular. A smaller *koshi* pattern was rotated 45 degrees (putting stitching lines on the diagonal) and then placed within a larger grid. The midsections of antique sashiko garments from the Aizu region of Japan use the pattern shown in design 1:7 to provide a visual break between more intricate designs at shoulder and hem. Other antique garments use this double *koshi* pattern to surround the *shippo* or *kaku-shippo* designs. (See designs 2:3 and 3:16.)

DIAMONDS

In modern Japanese, the word *hishi* describes the diamond shape that is formed when lines intersect with alternating 60-degree and 120-degree angles. (Originally, the word named a water chestnut plant with diamond-shaped leaves that grew in ponds and swamps in Japan.) One of the simplest sashiko diamond-shaped designs is the *hishi-moyo* (diamond) pattern, shown in design 1:8. To form the *hishi-moyo* design, a series of parallel diagonal lines is rotated 120 degrees and then superimposed on the original lines. The diamond shapes are wider than they are tall.

BAMBOO FENCE

When *hishi-moyo* is rotated 90 degrees (so that the diamond shapes are taller than they are wide as shown in design 1:9) it becomes *yarai* (bamboo fence). To illustrate how scale affects design, only every other line of the *hishi-moyo* shown in design 1:8 has been used in the rotated design 1:9. Both the *hishi-moyo* and the *yarai* designs are stitched off grain. To avoid stretching the fabric, sew from the center of the design outward and also alternate the direction in which each line is stitched.

PARALLEL DIAMONDS, AND CROSSED CORDS

The sashiko tradition includes many variations on *hishi-moyo*. The version shown in design 1:10 dates back to the Jomon period. In modern Japan, it has two alternate names: *hishi-igeta* (parallel diamonds) or *tasuki* (crossed cords). The *tasuki* name recalls the fact that this sashiko design resembles the pattern that the tasuki cord makes on the back of a kimono when it is used to tie sleeves out of the wearer's way. Like the variation of *koshi* presented in design 1:6, the design is enhanced by the introduction of unstitched space. Every other set of original lines has been skipped, but a close, parallel line has been added.

DESIGN 1:9
Yarai
BAMBOO FENCE

矢来

DESIGN 1:10
Hishi-Igeta and Tasuki
PARALLEL DIAMONDS AND CROSSED CORDS

菱井桁

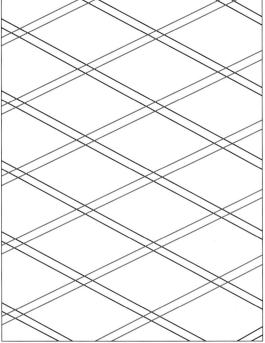

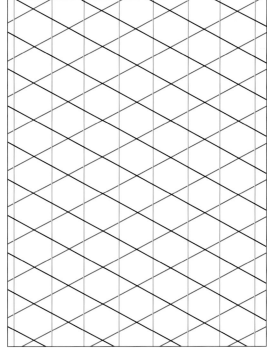

WOVEN BAMBOO

Other sashiko patterns build on the *hishi-moyo* design. For example, placing *tate-jima* (from design 1:1) over *hishi-moyo* (from design 1:8) forms the most typical version of *kagome* (woven bamboo) in design 1:11. Most variants of the *kagome* design place vertical lines over a crisscross pattern, and, often, the vertical lines are slightly farther apart than the crisscross lines.

WOVEN BAMBOO

Horizontal lines, however, are also used. To make a kagome pattern with horizontal lines, overlay *yoko-jima* (from design 1:3) on *yarai* (from design 1:9). The horizontal overlaid lines are the same distance apart as the crisscross lines, and this symmetry creates a six-pointed star resembling the Star of David (design 1:12). A six-pointed star forms in many sashiko patterns because the Japanese believed it to have magical attributes.

In all variants of the *kagome* pattern, the three sets of lines do not intersect at a single point. The *kagome* pattern is one of two widely used designs associated with the summer season. (The other is the *amime*, or fishing net.) *Kagome* stitching recalls the open weave of bamboo and paper lanterns that are frequently used outdoors in Japan during the summer.

WOVEN BAMBOO

Substituting double lines for the single lines in the horizontal *kagome* pattern produces another version of the popular six-pointed star (design 1:13). Because the double-stitched, off grain lines may stretch the fabric, stitch all the horizontal lines first. If your fabric starts to gather when you sew, your needle and bobbin tensions are balanced too tightly for your fabric/stabilizer combination. To correct, rebalance your tension at a lower setting for both the needle thread and the bobbin.

FISH SCALES

The *hishi-moyo* pattern is also a component of the *uroko* (fish scale) design. The version of *uroko* shown in design 1:14 is made in the same way that most versions of *kagome* are made: a basic *tate-jima* pattern is overlaid on a *hishi-moyo* pattern. In design 1:14, only every other line from *hishi-moyo* (design 1:8) and *tate-jima* (design 1:1) has been used.

Designs made from three intersecting lines date back to the Jomon period. Variants of the *uroko* design are probably among the oldest sashiko patterns. In Japan's early history, such designs were called *kyoshi* (saw-tooth). The design began to represent scales only during Japan's feudal period.

DESIGN 1:13
Kagome
WOVEN BAMBOO

籠目

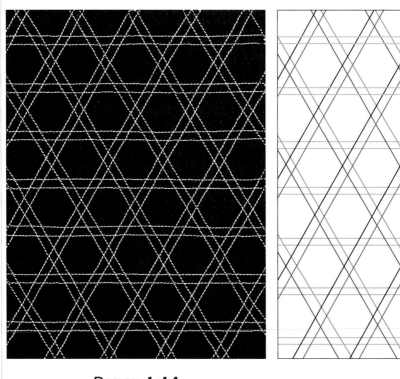

DESIGN 1:14
Uroko
FISH SCALES

鱗

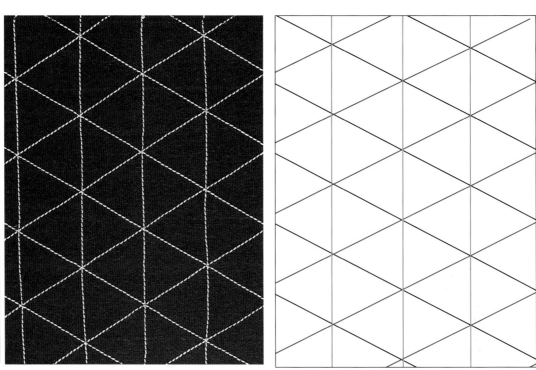

DESIGN 1:15
Mitsu-Uroko
FISH SCALES

密鱗

DESIGN 1:16
Uroko
FISH SCALES

鱗

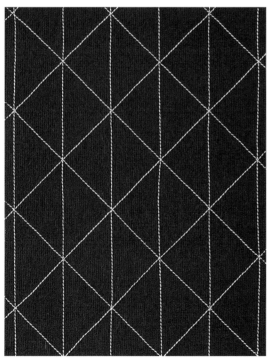

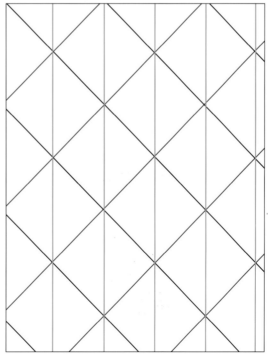

FISH SCALES

The variation of *uroko* called *mitsu-uroko* (design 1:15) places a *yoko-jima* pattern over a *yarai* pattern. In Noh and Kabuki theater costumes, the design symbolized the degeneration of a beautiful woman into a dreadful, jealous creature. At a play's beginning, a character would hide a *mitsu-uroko* kimono under another kimono. The character would later throw the outer kimono off, revealing the *mitsu-uroko* kimono to signify that the character had been corrupted by jealousy. The frequently produced "*Musume-dojo-ji*" play uses this imagery. In it, a young woman falls in love with a travelling monk. He fails to return to her as promised. She tracks him to his temple and ultimately turns herself into a snake in order to kill him. Although *uroko* is translated as fish scales, in most Japanese stories associated with the design, a snake or sea serpent, rather than a fish, leaves its scales behind.

FISH SCALES

A few versions of *uroko* (such as design 1:16) use a rotated *koshi* grid as a foundation rather than a *hishi-moyo* design. When a *koshi* pattern is used, the diagonal lines form 90-degree angles instead of alternating 60- and 120-degree angles. As always in *uroko* designs, all three lines intersect.

97

RISING STEAM

When a gently curved line is paired with its mirror image, the *tate-waku* (rising steam) design forms (design 2:1). Paintings of Japanese court life show the *tate-waku* design on ceremonial robes as early as the Heian period. By the Edo period, *tate-waku* was used as a framework for many textile patterns. Flowers or other circular motifs were placed inside the convex areas in the design. Commoners adapted the pattern for sashiko. Antique sashiko-embellished kimonos show both single-line and double-line versions of the design. Sashiko projects in modern Japanese books sometimes play on the association of the design with rising steam, such as using the design to embellish potholders.

COUNTERWEIGHTS

Fundo (counterweights) in design 2:2 uses similar, but more deeply curved, mirror-imaged lines. A second set of lines is placed over the first set at a right angle. The entire design is always shown on the diagonal. The *fundo* design was popularized during the Edo period when an effort was made to develop purely Japanese designs. Many objects from everyday Japanese life, such as the counterweights used in market balancescales, were elevated as design motifs.

DESIGN 2:1
Tate-Waku
RISING STEAM

堅沸く

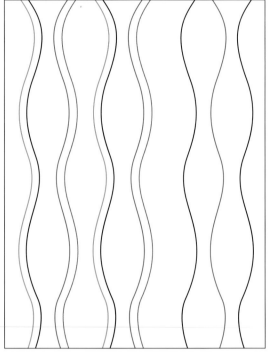

DESIGN 2:2
Fundo
COUNTERWEIGHTS

分銅

DESIGN 2:3
Shippo
THE SEVEN TREASURES OF BUDDHA

七宝

THE SEVEN TREASURES OF BUDDHA

The *shippo* pattern of interconnected circles has long been used in Buddhist art. Calling the design "seven treasures of Buddha" may have originated from a pun on the ideograph that named the design. According to John W. Dower in his book *The Elements of Japanese Design*, the ideograph literally translates as "four directions" but could also be read as "seven treasures." The seven treasures of Buddha are gold, silver, lapis, agate, pearl, coral, and crystal. (Amber is occasionally substituted for crystal.) The *shippo* design probably entered Japan during the Asuka period along with Buddhism. Antique sashiko-embellished garments show several variations on the design: a diagonal or a vertical/horizontal *koshi* grid, or both (like design 1:7), may be overlaid on the basic *shippo* design. These overlays are shown in the stitching on the lower portion of design 2:3.

DESIGN 2:4
Shippo
THE SEVEN TREASURES OF BUDDHA

七宝

THE SEVEN TREASURES OF BUDDHA

Another variant (design 2:4) leaves one side of the circle incomplete. These two designs illustrate one intrinsic difference between hand sewing and machine sewing. Following small s-curves may work best for a hand sewer, but most machine sewers will achieve better results if they follow large s-curves.

99

FISHING NET

The same design line forms both *amime* (upper portion of design 2:5) and *chidori* (design 2:6). In *amime*, the design line is mirror-imaged. In *chidori* the design line is rotated 90 degrees.

The *amime* (fishing net) design symbolizes summer in modern Japan. It decorates ceramics and lacquerware as well as textiles. The design was elevated during the Edo period as an intrinsically Japanese motif. Because they live on an island, the Japanese give special significance to motifs associated with the ocean. As the lower portion of design 2:5 shows, the *amime* design is also drawn in an elongated fashion. Both versions of the design are attractive, and mixing them in a single article of clothing or home fashions is more attractive still.

PLOVERS

Chidori symbolizes autumn. First used as a design motif during the Heian period, it represents a species of sea bird found in Japan. The design's association with autumn may reflect the migration pattern of these birds. *Chidori* translates as a "thousand birds" but is usually called "plovers" in English. The red stitching on *chidori* (design 2:6) hints why *toridasuki* (design 2:7) is given the English name "interconnected circle of two birds."

DESIGN 2:5
Amime
FISHING NET

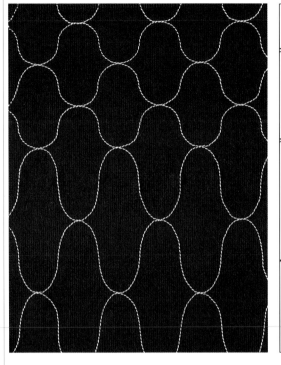

網目

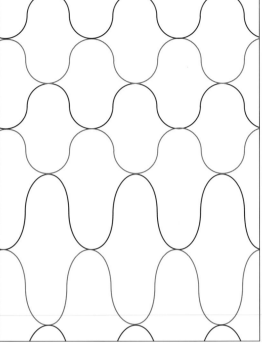

DESIGN 2:6
Chidori
PLOVER

千鳥

DESIGN 2:7
Toridasuki
INTERLACED CIRCLE OF TWO BIRDS

鳥襷

DESIGN 2:8
Shippo
OVAL SHAPED SEVEN TREASURES

七宝

INTERLACED CIRCLE OF TWO BIRDS

The *toridasuki* pattern forms when one *chidori* pattern overlaps another. Design 2:7 can also be formed by rotating an *amime* pattern 90 degrees and overlaying it on a second, unrotated *amime*. If you have trouble "seeing" this, you may want to sew the small wall hanging project beginning on page 69 which was specifically designed to have you construct the *toridasuki* pattern by both possible routes.

To further understand how a single design line creates very different patterns, also look at the large s-curve in design 2:3. Although it is scaled differently, *shippo* uses the same curved line that *amime*, *chidori*, and *toridasuki* patterns also use.

OVAL-SHAPED SEVEN TREASURES

If this realization didn't strike you, you can develop your skill in recognizing how line segments build designs by stitching the oval-shaped *shippo* pattern in design 2:8. Although the curves are elongated, you should feel exactly the same "rhythm" when you stitch this line that you feel when stitching the lines of *amime*, *chidori*, and *toridasuki*.

MIST

Because mountainous terrain frequently causes mist, clouds of mist are prominent in Japanese landscapes dating back to the Asuka period. The *kasumi* (mist) pattern (design 2:9) used in sashiko is subtle and has a long repeat. In order for the design to be seen, it has to be stitched either with very tight curves, or, if enlarged, stitched over a very large area. Modern Japanese-produced or inspired textiles resolve this difficulty by enlarging *kasumi* and printing other traditional textile patterns within the design's interior. This design strategy echoes a traditional use of mist to signal a break between time periods or physical locations in otherwise representational paintings. If you find that the *kasumi* pattern is too difficult to stitch in the scale shown because of its extremely tight curves, borrow this strategy and use *kasumi* as the "frame" for a large wall hanging that showcases many other sashiko designs.

UNTITLED HOKUSAI #1

Fortunately, Hokusai developed a design that has somewhat the same "feel" as the *kasumi* pattern, but which is much easier to stitch. It is reproduced as design 2:10. You may wish to substitute this pattern for the *kasumi* pattern in some projects.

DESIGN 2:9
Kasumi
MIST

霞

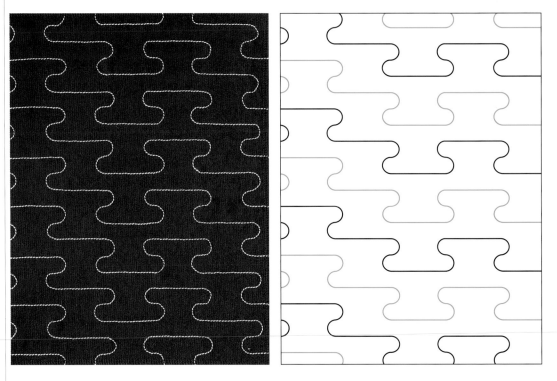

DESIGN 2:10
Untitled Hokusai #1
北斉-無題

DESIGN 2:11
Asanoha
HEMP LEAF (HOKUSAI'S VERSION, SIMPLIFIED)

麻の葉

DESIGN 2:12
Mitsuba
TREFOIL PATTERN BY HOKUSAI

三葉

HEMP LEAF

Because cotton fabrics took longer to become affordable and available to residents of northern Japan, hemp clothing continued to be used well into the 18th century in those regions. A distinctive style of sashiko called *kogin* developed to take advantage of the short cotton threads that were available. Undyed threads were so intensively woven into sections of the indigo-colored hemp garments that they became predominately white. Since cotton is a far better insulator than hemp, this made clothing warmer. Often *kogin* was stitched only on the top of a garment. The lower parts, which wore out faster, were replaced and reattached to the top. The persimmon blossom and the hemp leaf were particularly popular motifs. The *asanoha* (hemp leaf) pattern is usually stitched with straight lines and pivots. However, the artist Hokusai introduced a version that was composed of curved lines. In design 2:11, Hokusai's pattern was slightly modified to allow for continuous stitching.

TREFOIL PATTERN

Design 2:12 is another Hokusai pattern. Modern Japanese books identify it as *mitsuba* (trefoil) pattern. The shape formed by this pattern is used by many Christian denominations to represent the Trinity and is called the "triquetra."

RISING STEAM/FISHING NET

Hokusai was fond of mixing two different patterns together. A representative example is shown in design 2:13. Hokusai may have intended the design to symbolize the "steam" that the ocean gives off in the morning when the water temperature is higher than the air temperature, a sight that often greets fisherman as they set out in the early morning. Alternatively, because its curved horizontal lines resemble *fundo* as well as *tate waku*, the design may have symbolized fishermen returning at the end of the day to weigh their catch. Or, through its ambiguity, it may have even symbolized both the beginning and the end of the day of fishing. Of course, it is also possible (though much less intriguing a thought) that Hokusai developed the design just because it was a pleasing combination of two shapes. Nevertheless, if you (or your significant other) is a fisherman, this design would be perfect to use to quilt a warm vest to wear on fishing trips.

SIX-SIDED FLOWER

Another pattern by Hokusai appears as design 2:14. It looks so modern that it may be somewhat shocking to learn that it was published in 1824.

DESIGN 2:13
Tate Waku/Amime
COMPOSITE RISING STEAM/FISHING NET PATTERN

竪沸く

DESIGN 2:14
Untitled Hokusai #2
SIX-SIDED FLOWER PATTERN BY HOKUSAI

北斉-無題

DESIGN 3:1
Dan and Yama Sashi
CONNECTED STEPS (UPPER PART OF SAMPLE)
MOUNTAINS (LOWER PART OF SAMPLE)

段

DESIGN 3:2
Hirayama-Michi
PASSES IN THE MOUNTAINS

山刺し

CONNECTED STEPS MOUNTAINS

Some of the oldest sashiko design lines use pivots that Japanese commoners originally stitched by counting warp and weft threads on coarse hemp fabric. In the two patterns shown in design 3:1, stitching moves diagonally across the fabric because pivots turn downward and sideways. When the diagonal rows are stitched the same distance apart as the line segments are long, the design is called *dan* (connected steps). When the rows are sewn closer (with only half that distance separating them), the design represents mountains called *yama*. The difference in the two designs shows how important unstitched space is to overall appearance.

PASSES IN THE MOUNTAINS

Design 3.2 shows a variation on the yama design called *hirayama-michi* (passes in the mountains). Changing the design line to pivot alternately up and down after sideways pivots creates this entirely different pattern. A diagonal pattern thus changes into a horizontal one, and an asymmetrical pattern turns into a symmetrical one. The very bottom of design 3.2 shows another design variation. The horizontal line segments now turn up after two sideways pivots, then down after two sideways pivots. This line is the basis for the *kaki* (persimmon) pattern.

PERSIMMON FLOWER BORDER DESIGN

When rows of the *kaki* pattern are sewn so they mirror-image each other, the outline of the border variant of the *kaki no hana* (persimmon flower) is formed. Design 3:3 shows how to complete *kaki no hana* design by sewing a square in the middle of the pattern. Use of this motif in Japan dates to the Nara period. The persimmon fruit was celebrated for its beauty, and on New Year's day an offering of the fruit was made to the gods.

PERSIMMON FLOWER BORDER DESIGN

Another common sashiko pattern, called *juji*, also uses right-angle pivots but has different length line segments. In English, it is called both "tens" (because the pattern resembles the Japanese ideogram for the number ten) and "connected crosses." The basic design line (shown in black) always turns down after each sideways pivot, causing the stitching to move diagonally as in the *dan* and *yama sashi* patterns. To form the pattern shown in design 3:4, a second set of lines (shown in red) is rotated 90 degrees and placed over the first set. Horizontal segments in the design line are twice the length of vertical segments, whereas the reverse is true in the rotated line.

DESIGN 3:3
Kaki No Hana
PERSIMMON FLOWER BORDER DESIGN

柿の花

DESIGN 3:4
Juji
TENS OR CONNECTED CROSSES

十字

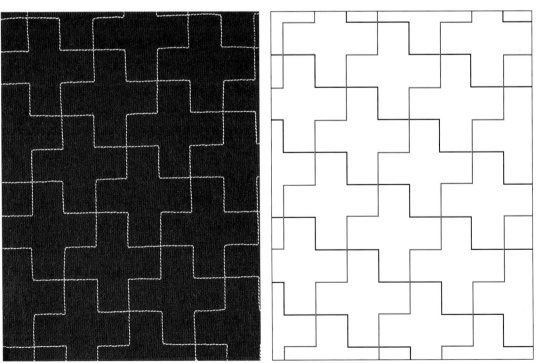

DESIGN 3:5
Untitled Hokusai #3

北斉-無題

DESIGN 3:6
Kaki No Hana
PERSIMMON FLOWER

柿の花

The artist Hokusai created a new design by increasing the length of the vertical line segment in design 3:3 and then rotating and overlaying this line on itself. The resultant design, shown in design 3:5, resembles pieces of jigsaw puzzle fitted together.

PERSIMMON FLOWER

Design 3:6 is another traditional version of the persimmon flower pattern. The line moves down after each pivot like the *dan* and *yama* patterns shown in design 3:1. But in this design, every other vertical line segment is twice as long. Because the design line (shown in black) always turn down after each horizontal segment, the stitching moves diagonally. As in the *juji* pattern in design 3:4, a second set of lines is rotated 90 degrees and overlaid over the first set, forming a pattern of six-sided crosses. The *kaki no hana* design is completed by sewing a square in the middle of each cross. Some antique sashiko-embellished garments use multiple stitching lines for the *kaki no hana* design as is shown by the red stitching.

GEOMETRICAL PATTERN FROM CHINA

Some sashiko patterns are made by fitting two pivoting lines inside each other. The Japanese call the double-line pattern in design 3:7 *kanmon*. This pattern also occurs in textiles produced by many cultures, including the molas sewn by the Cuna Indians of Panama. This very symmetrical pattern came to Japan by way of China, as did many other early sashiko designs. Like *hirayama-michi* of design 3:2, the pivots in *kanmon* move it horizontally, making it an excellent border design. Multiple repeats of the *kanmon* pattern can also fill a wider expanse of cloth as design 3:7 illustrates.

THUNDERBOLTS

Changing the direction of a pivot, this time at the design's lower edge, creates the pattern shown in design 3:8. The design now moves diagonally like the dan and yama *sashi*. Diagonal double lines often represented thunderbolts, known as *kaminari*. Costumes in Noh plays used thunderbolt patterns to signify the wearer's power and authority. Although this design is as easy to sew as *kanmon*, it looks more complex because of its asymmetry.

DESIGN 3:7
Kanmon
GEOMETRICAL PATTERN FROM CHINA

漢文

DESIGN 3:8
Kaminari
THUNDERBOLTS

雷

DESIGN 3:9
Manji
MANJI PATTERN #1 BY HOKUSAI

まん字

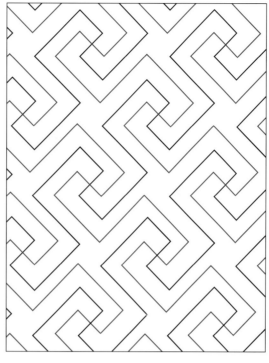

DESIGN 3:10
Untitled
PATTERN FROM ANTIQUE KIMONOS

無題

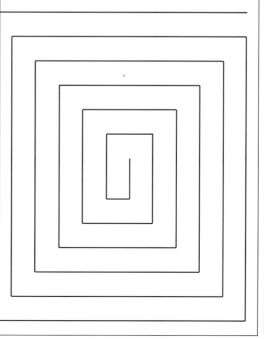

MANJI PATTERN #1 BY HOKUSAI

The artist Hokusai produced the pattern shown in design 3:9 based on the *manji*, or Buddhist cross. The design line strongly resembles that of the *kaminari* pattern in design 3:8. But Hokusai's design looks quite different because his slightly different pattern of pivots breaks the double line effect found in both *kanmon* and *kaminari*.

PATTERN FROM ANTIQUE KIMONOS

The sashiko stitching on many antique kimonos in Japanese museums forms a pattern like that shown in design 3:10. The design in the very center of the pattern varies slightly from kimono to kimono. The very simplest version is shown here. Other versions begin the stitching in the center with a triangle or square. This pattern is not commonly used in modern sashiko, so it is difficult to tell what the design meant to those who stitched it on their garments so long ago. Decorative motifs almost always had a specific meaning for the Japanese. Designs were not used as abstract embellishment but were instead used to convey particular meanings.

LIGHTNING

A pattern called *inazuma* is used in sashiko to represent lightning. Like the *kanmon* design, it came to Japan from China. This pattern makes a single line pivot back on itself in such a way that it appears to be a double line. Both versions shown in design 3:11 use right angle pivots, but the second is made to look diamond-shaped by stitching on the diagonal. In addition to being useful as a border for household linens, both patterns make an excellent placket treatment for a blouse or an attractive skirt border.

SILK WEAVE OR KEY PATTERN

The *sayagata* (called the key or silk weave pattern) is based upon much the same construction principles as the *kanmon* pattern. The *sayagata* segment uses a more complex pattern of up/down and left/right pivots. However, as design 3:12 shows, it is easily stitched. The black design line moves horizontally, as in *kanmon*. As in *juji*, a second set of lines (shown in red) is rotated, then overlaid on the set of design lines. The *sayagata* has a long and interesting history. The design apparently originated in Greece, but traveled along the silk road into India, where it became associated with Buddhism. It found its way to China, and was eventually introduced into Japan, both through Japan's importing of Chinese silk textiles that used this design and through the influence of Buddhism.

DESIGN 3:11
Inazuma
LIGHTNING

稲光

DESIGN 3:12
Sayagata
SILK WEAVE OR KEY PATTERN

鞘型

DESIGN 3:13
Manji
MANJI PATTERN #2 BY HOKUSAI

まん字

DESIGN 3:14
Hishi-sayagata
DIAMOND SHAPED SILK WEAVE OR KEY PATTERN

菱鞘型

The artist Hokusai also produced a pattern (design 3:13) based on the *manji*, or Buddhist cross, with a design line that strongly resembles the sayagata's design line.

DIAMOND-SHAPED SILK WEAVE OR KEY PATTERN

Not all pivots in sashiko are right angles. Perhaps the most well known example of alternating 60- and 120-degree pivots is the *hishi-sayagata* (diamond-shaped silk weave) pattern shown in design 3:14. The 60 degree/120 degree angles make the design travel on a diagonal, rather than on vertical and horizontal axes, making it appear much more sophisticated and difficult to stitch than the right-angled *sayagata*. However, in reality, *hishi-sayagata* is no more difficult to stitch that the right-angled version.

Both *sayagata* and *hishi-sayagata* designs can be seen in Japanese museums' collections of antique, sashiko-stitched peasant clothing in which multiple lines may even shadow the single line used in the original design. In modern Japan, *hishi-sayagata* may be the most popular of all sashiko designs.

PINE BARK

The *matsukawa-bishi* (pine bark) pattern shown in design 3:15 also uses alternating 60- and 120-degree pivots. Line segments turn down, moving the stitching diagonally like the *juji* pattern. The *matsukawa-bishi* looks so different from *juji* primarily because the pivot angles on its design line are different and because the second set of lines is mirror-imaged rather than rotated. The construction principles of the two patterns are really very much the same.

Because the pine remained green throughout the very cold Japanese winters, this design became a symbol of perseverance and good fortune. The motif was popularized through costumes worn in the Noh theater. In Japanese restaurants in this country, waitresses will often wear a kimono with the *matsukawa-bishi* design in the winter and switch to a kimono with the *amime* design in the summer. The two designs effectively complement each other and are well-understood symbols of the winter and summer seasons, respectively.

PINE BARK BY HOKUSAI

Hokusai embellished the basic *matsukawa-bishi* pattern as shown in design 3:16. It is more challenging to stitch than design 3:15 because irregularities caused by stitches not calibrated to the shortest line segment are much more apparent. However, the additional sophistication of this design makes it worth the trouble to be precise.

DESIGN 3:15
Matsukawa-Bishi
PINE BARK

松皮菱

DESIGN 3:16
Matsukawa-Bishi
PINE BARK BY HOKUSAI

松皮菱

DESIGN 3:17
Yabane
ARROW-FEATHERS

矢羽

DESIGN 3:18
Kaku-Shippo
ANGLED OR DIAMOND-SHAPED SEVEN TREASURES

角七宝

ARROW-FEATHERS

Design 3:17 is one of several distinctive designs in modern sashiko that all bear the name *yabane* (arrow-feathers). In much the same way that Western culture has romanticized the long sword as representing the epitome of chivalrous combat, Japanese view the bow and arrow as the embodiment of their own warrior tradition. Even today, the Zen sect of Buddhism emphasizes training in archery as a way for men to develop mediation skills. (Women, on the other hand, are encouraged to practice the art of flower arranging, known as *ikebana*.)

ANGLED OR DIAMOND-SHAPED SEVEN TREASURES

Because the diamond and the circle were both favorite shapes for family crests, many Japanese designs exist in both circular and diamond-shaped versions. When the smooth curves of *shippo* design were drawn instead as two straight line segments with a pivot between them, a new pattern called *kaku-shippo* (angled or diamond-shaped seven treasures) was created. As shown in design 3:18, vertical/horizontal and/or diagonal *koshi* grids were often superimposed over this basic diamond-shaped design. The diagonal *koshi* grid is overlaid on the right and the horizontal/vertical *koshi* grid on the left. Both grids overlay the center.

ANGLED OR DIAMOND-SHAPED SEVEN TREASURES AND SEA URCHIN

Additional pivoting lines enhance the *kaku-shippo* pattern. In more complex examples, up to seven lines appear in each diamond, as shown in design 3:19. The design was further transformed on the island of Tobishima as some or all of the interior lines were sewn as circular arcs rather than as straight-line pivots. Here the design also lost its association with the original *shippo* pattern from which it was morphed, and was referred to simply as the sea urchin pattern. This variant on the basic multi-line design is shown at the very bottom of design 3:19. It is ironic that although the design at least partially transformed back to its original shape, it lost its original meaning.

UNTITLED HOKUSAI #4

Although the pattern reproduced as design 3:20 bears some resemblance to the *kaku-shippo* pattern shown in design 3:18, it may have had a very different origin. Intersection points are clearly formed from six equally spaced lines, not just four. The most common Japanese pattern that has six intersecting lines at its center is the *asanoha* (hemp leaf). The design may therefore represent an abstraction and extension of the basic hemp leaf pattern. Hokusai introduced this pattern in his 1824 book of designs.

DESIGN 3:19
Kaku-Shippo & Uni
ANGLED OR DIAMOND-SHAPED SEVEN TREASURES AND SEA URCHIN

角七宝 AND 雲丹

DESIGN 3:20
Untitled Hokusai #4

北斉-無題

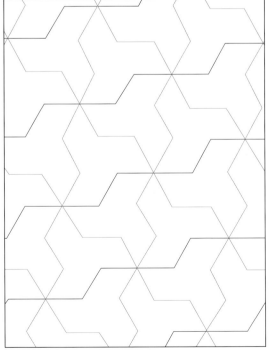

DESIGN 3:21
Untitled Hokusai #5

北斉-無題

DESIGN 3:22
Untitled Pattern
FROM ANTIQUE KIMONOS PROBABLY VARIANT OF ASA

無題

UNTITLED HOKUSAI #5

In his 1824 book, Hokusai also took the pattern in design 3:20 one step further. Additional pivots are added, and the design is elongated. The resultant design, reproduced as design 3:21, looks intricate, but is very easy to stitch.

UNTITLED PATTERN FROM ANTIQUE KIMONOS, PROBABLY VARIANT OF ASA

The pattern shown in design 3:22 is found on an antique kimono from the Shizuoka Municipal Serizawa Keisuke Art Museum. It is almost certainly an abstraction of the basic hemp leaf, or *asa*, design. Several *mon*, or family crests, that use the traditional hemp leaf design, show half of its six leaves in black and the other half in white. The black leaves form exactly the same pattern used on this kimono. The design is particularly interesting in that it forms a six-pointed star.

LIGHTNING

Representations of lightning were not only stitched with right angles, such as those shown in design 3:11, but also with pairs of oblique/acute angles, such as shown in design 3:23. The *inazuma* designs apparently pre-date their association with lightning. According to John W. Dower in his book *The Elements of Japanese Design,* the ideograph for *inazuma* is literally translated as "rice-plant wife." Mr. Dower believes that this name suggests the design may have originally symbolized "fecundity and the basic forces of life."

CROSS AND CHECK PATTERN BY HOKUSAI

Design 3:24 is yet another developed by Hokusai. He enlivened the basic *koshi* grid by introducing *manji* designs at each intersection.

DESIGN 3:23
Inazuma
LIGHTNING

稲光

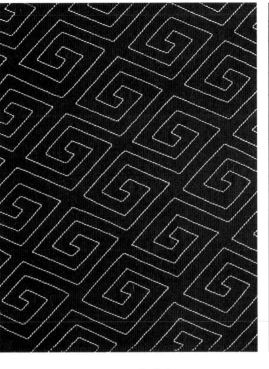

DESIGN 3:24
Manji-Koshi
CROSS AND CHECK PATTERN BY HOKUSAI

まん字格子

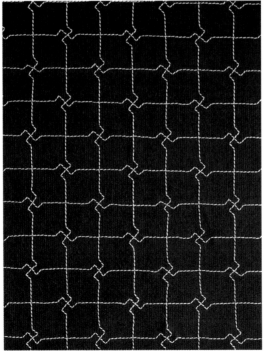

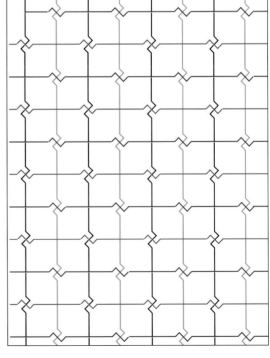

Design 4:1
Seigaiha
Blue Ocean Waves

青海波

Overlapping wave designs are called *seigaiha*, which means blue ocean waves. In the Japanese design, representations of the ceaseless motion of waves on the ocean symbolize eternity and immortality.

Because all the arcs in design 4:1 converge at the same point, it is easy to stitch the curves continuously if your stitch length is correctly calibrated. Each arc can be sewn in a different thread color (as shown on the color-coded pattern) if desired. The double-arc form of this design is shown at the top, and a triple-arc form that I developed is shown at the bottom.

Design 4:2
Seigaiha
Blue Ocean Waves

青海波

BLUE OCEAN WAVES

Design 4:2 requires pivoting from the large arcs onto the smaller "sideways crescent moon" shape when the two colors meet in the pattern. After sewing the upper arc of the smaller "sideways crescent moon," pivot and sew the lower arc. This completes the "sideways crescent moon" and returns you to your original position on the large arc. Continue stitching on the larger arc.

COMMA SHAPE

The *tomoe*, or comma shape, resembles the shape of the leather band (*tomo*) that a Japanese archer would wear to protect the left wrist. The design came to be associated with the god of war, Hachiman, and developed widespread popularity as a family crest during Japan's long feudal period. However, similar designs are also found in Chinese art, which may explain why the design has a alternative history as a charm against penetration of water. In Japan, the roofs of temples were often decorated with *tomoe* motifs to ward off leaks. My original *tomoe* pattern (design 4:3) emphasizes the whirlpool aspect that was thought to draw water away. This design would be especially appropriate for quilting the lining of a waterproof outerwear garment.

CONNECTED SEMICIRCLES

The *hanmaru* pattern (design 4:4) builds upon the *toridasuki* (design 2:7). The wall hanging project on page 69 provides a step-by-step look at how the design is constructed. Although it looks complex, it is actually easy to stitch if the color coding is followed.

DESIGN 4:3
Tomoe
COMMA SHAPE (ORIGINAL DESIGN)

巴

DESIGN 4:4
Hanmaru
CONNECTED SEMICIRCLES

半丸

DESIGN 4:5
Nowaki
BLOWING PAMPAS GRASS

野脇

DESIGN 4:6
Icho
GINGKO LEAF (ORIGINAL DESIGN)

銀杏

BLOWING PAMPAS GRASS

The *nowaki* (pampas grass) symbolizes autumn. The surrounding semicircles in design 4:5 are not clamshells, but a wave pattern called *nami*. The Japanese often use *nami* as a frame. To sew the *nowaki* design, stitch the blades of grass as you begin each large *nami* arc. Blades can be sewn either by pivoting between the two small converging arcs (as the design is drawn) or by stitching a single arc twice. To sew the single arc, simply lift your presser foot after you have completed sewing one small arc and turn your fabric completely around. Then sew back to your original point on the *nami* arc by stitching in exactly the same needle holes.

GINGKO LEAF

My original pattern in design 4:6 for *icho* (gingko tree leaf) also uses a *nami* frame. The name of the gingko tree gave rise to another pun. According to John W. Dower, in his book *The Elements of Japanese Design*, the ideograph for the gingko reads "duck's foot tree," a reference to the shape of the gingko leaf. However, the spoken name could also be understood as "barbarians bring tribute."

When sewing designs embedded in *nami* arcs, skip some of them, as shown in designs 4:5 and 4:6. Creative use of unsewn space is very much in keeping with the Japanese aesthetic taste.

WISTERIA BORDER DESIGN BY HOKUSAI

Wisteria, called *fuji* by the Japanese, originally grew wild in the area near Kyoto and Osaka. Mount Fuji is even named for the plant. The beauty of the *fuji* (wisteria) is celebrated in literature of the Nara period. The design continued to be favored well into the Edo period. Hokusai included a *fuji* motif (design 4:7) in his 1824 book of designs for craftsmen. Because the shape of the petals is somewhat similar, the *fuji* motif may sometimes be confused with the *tessen* (clematis) pattern. Design 4:8 shows the characteristic petal shape of *tessen*. Whereas the *fuji* petal is absolutely symmetrical, the *tessen* petal shape is asymmetrical, with the left node being much larger than the right node.

CLEMATIS (ORIGINAL DESIGN)

My original *tessen* pattern is a continuous border design, but stitching multiple rows will fill in wider areas. First stitch the lines on the color-coded pattern whose color is also used for the circle in the center of the flower. Sew the circle immediately when your stitching first reaches the interior of the flower. Then sew individual petals, with your stitches just touching the inner circle as you pivot onto the next petal. The second stitching line that completes each flower also just touches the previously sewn circle as it pivots between the other petals.

DESIGN 4:7
Fuji
WISTERIA BORDER DESIGN BY HOKUSAI

藤

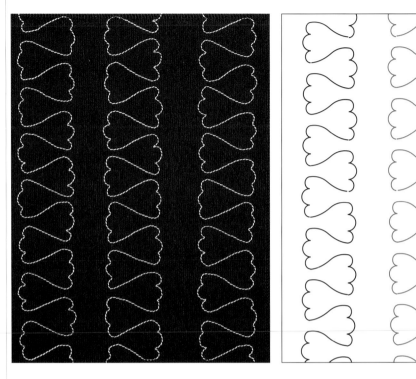

DESIGN 4:8
Tessen
CLEMATIS (ORIGINAL DESIGN)

鉄線

DESIGN 4:9
Hanabishi
DIAMOND-SHAPED FLOWER

花菱

DESIGN 4:10
Nashi
PEAR BLOSSOM (ORIGINAL DESIGN)

梨

DIAMOND-SHAPED FLOWER

A diamond-shaped flower design, called *hanabishi*, translates literally as "flower diamond." The stitching in the *hanabishi* pattern in design 4:9 moves diagonally. A single diagonal row would be attractive when sewn over a large area, such as in a window curtain, if a sophisticated, diagonally striped motif was desired. First stitch the curved lines marked in the colors that form the half-circles in the center of the flowers. When you reach the point of a loop on each half-circle, pivot and sew the entire loop. You will return to the same point, and you can then complete sewing the half-circle. When you sew the other lines in the design, simply touch the circle as you pivot between the petals.

PEAR BLOSSOM (ORIGINAL DESIGN)

The stitching pattern for the *nashi* (pear blossom) of design 4:10 is similar. In addition to making half of a large petal, one line also makes the four smaller petals, pivoting out from and returning to the center point after each. Another line, in addition to making half of another large petal, makes the four stamens, pivoting in and out from the center point in exactly the same manner. The other two lines simply pass through the center point of the design. Historians believe that the basic pattern underlying design 4:10 is an abstracted flower shape that existed long before it became associated with the pear.

WOOD SORREL

As the presence of sword-shapes in the *katabami* (wood sorrel) of design 4:11 suggests, the design developed during Japan's feudal period. The warrior class particularly favored the design because the plant was so prolific. The emblem signified their expectation that their descendants would enlarge the family's territory as readily as the wood sorrel took over a field. The pattern originated in the late Heian period, but came into its greatest vogue later.

CHINESE FLOWER

Design 4:12 uses the *karabana* (Chinese flower) which was among the very earliest designs used on Japanese textiles. As the name implies, the design came from China. The *karakana* is presented last in this section because its stitching requires the most precision. The interior circle is implied rather than stitched. The circle appears only if the pivots at the center of the design are all made exactly on the implied center circle. The *hanabishi* design shown on the preceding page represents a Japanese adaptation of the original five-petaled *karabana* design into a four-petal form to allow it to be displayed within a *hishi-moyo* framework. Even though the four petal, diamond-shaped *hanabishi* design was a fairly early invention, its popularity lasted into the Edo period, where it was often further transformed into a square. By alternating the design with a blank square, a checkerboard textile design was produced.

DESIGN 4:11
Katabami
WOOD SORREL (ORIGINAL DESIGN)

酢漿草

DESIGN 4:12
Karabana
CHINESE FLOWER (ORIGINAL DESIGN)

唐花

DESIGN 5:1
Kasane Kikko
OVERLAPPING TORTOISESHELLS

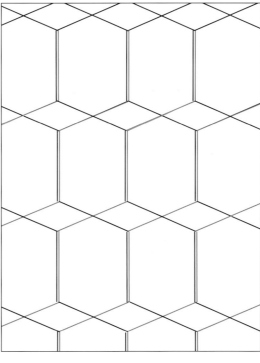

DESIGN 5:2
Tsumiki or Hako-Zashi
CHILD'S BUILDING BLOCKS OR STACKED BOXES

積木

OVERLAPPING TORTOISESHELLS

The *kasane kikko* (overlapping tortoiseshells) pattern shown in design 5:1 appears not only in Hokusai's 1824 book of designs, but also in other pattern books from the Edo period. A multitude of different *kikko* (tortoiseshell) designs have been popular in Japan since the Heian period. *Kikko* is always a hexagonal design. To sew *kasane kikko* easily, calibrate your stitch so that you hit the intersection points dead on. Your stitches will then automatically drop into the same needle holes both times the vertical line segments are stitched.

CHILD'S BUILDING BLOCKS OR STACKED BOXES

The *kasane kikko* serves as a basis for other sashiko designs. For example, the pattern known as *tsumiki* (child's building blocks) or *hako-zashi* (stacked boxes) is formed from two offset and overlaid *kasane kikko* patterns. If this isn't clear to you from looking at the color coding on the pattern for design 5:2, you may want to sew the crib quilt project beginning on page 75. This project leads you step by step through the design formation. Modern sashiko includes several variants of the *tsumiki/hako-zashi* pattern. Either one or two lines may be stitched on the "faces" of the blocks. These variations are shown in red thread on the sample. The single-line version even has its own name, *yosegiri* (marquetry).

As shown in design 5:3, *uroko* and *tsumiki/hako-zashi* combine to form one of the most popular of all sashiko designs, *asanoha* (hemp leaf). If the color coding does not show this clearly for you, you may want to sew the project beginning on page 75 to build the design first hand. Like many other sashiko designs, *asanoha* has strong associations with Buddhism. During the Heian period, paintings often show Buddha clothed in fabric patterned with an *asanoha* design. By the Edo period, however, the textile pattern had been virtually taken over by actors and fans of the Kabuki theater. Antique sashiko-embellished garments also often use the *asanoha* design, perhaps expressing a wish that the wearer would survive the winter, as the perennial hemp plant did. In modern Japan, the *asanoha* design is often sewn on garments for infants and small children, conveying the wish that the child will grow as vigorously and be as strong as the hemp plant.

HYDRANGEA

The same basic line that formed *tsumiki/hako-zashi* also forms *ajisai* (hydrangea, design 5:4). The relative length of the individual line segments has been changed and the second set of lines is rotated 90 degrees rather than simply being offset. It is this 90-degree rotation that gives the *ajisai* such a different look than the *tsumiki/hako-zashi*. The *ajisai* design is associated with summer.

DESIGN 5:3
Asanoha
HEMP LEAF

麻の葉

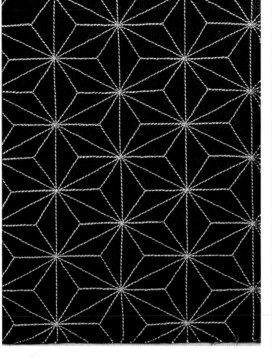

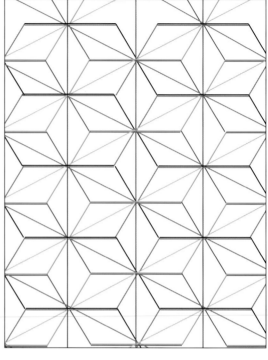

DESIGN 5:4
Ajisai
HYDRANGEA

紫陽花

DESIGN 5:5
Kikko
TORTOISESHELL

亀甲

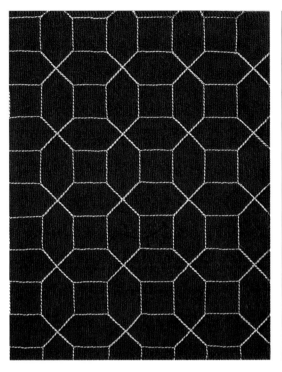

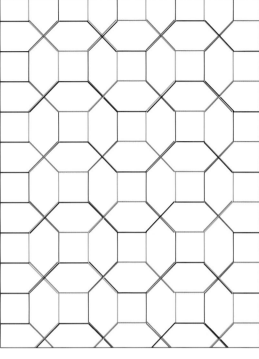

DESIGN 5:6
Igeta Ni Hakkaku
WATER WELLS

井桁に八角

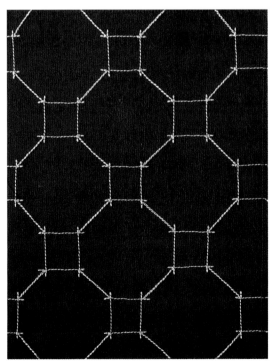

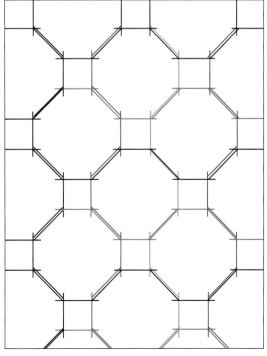

TORTOISESHELL

The tortoise remained a symbol of longevity when the motif traveled from China to Japan. Other sashiko patterns also symbolize longevity, such as *tsuru* (the crane), *kiku* (the chrysanthemum), and *matsu* (the pine tree), but *kikko* (tortoiseshell) motifs are the most powerful. Other symbols often convey a wish for only 1,000 years of life. However, the tortoise of ancient Chinese legends supported the heavens on its back for 10,000 years. Look for *kikko's* hexagonal shape in design 5:5.

WATER WELLS

Because all *kikko* patterns are hexagonal, novice students of Japanese design may think that all hexagonal patterns represent the tortoise. This is not true, as the *igeta ni hakkaku* pattern in design 5:6 demonstrates. Japanese readily recognize the design as *igeta* (a well crib). Well cribs are enclosures built around open wells as a safety measure that often supports pulleys to lower and raise water buckets). "I" is the first letter of the Japanese alphabet, and an *igeta* crest pattern is often used to help Japanese children learn their alphabet.

Both patterns are easy to stitch if you calibrate your stitch length correctly. The small extensions at the end of each side of the square in the *igeta* design are stitched by pivoting and taking two stitches forward and two stitches back before beginning to sew the actual side of the square.

Juji hanabishi translates literally as "diamond flower cross," but the pattern shown in design 5:7 is usually called blossoms in English. The design is sewn with the same line as the *kikko* pattern on the preceding page. The line is smaller-scaled in *juji hanabishi* and sewn on the diagonals of the fabric instead of the horizontal and vertical axes. However, as we saw when we compared *tsumiki/hako-zashi* (design 5:2) with *ajisai* (design 5:4), the fact the line is rotated 90 degrees in one design and not in the other produces a major difference in appearance. In the *juji hanabishi*, the lines are mirror-imaged rather than rotated 90 degrees as they were in *kikko*. Stitch small crosses in the center of each flower to mimic the look of stamens by dropping your needle in the exact center of the cross, sewing four stitches on a horizontal or vertical axis, turning your fabric around, and stitching back to the center. Repeat for all four axes, then bring threads through to the wrong side and knot.

BISHAMON

The version of *bishamon* shown in design 5:8 uses a similar line, although the angle of pivots is altered. Like *juji hanabishi*, the pattern is completed by a separate figure in the center. *Bishamon* is one of seven Chinese gods of good fortune. He represents wealth and is patron of doctors, soldiers, and priests. The textile patterns called *bishamon* were

DESIGN 5:7
Juji Hanabishi
BLOSSOM

十字花菱

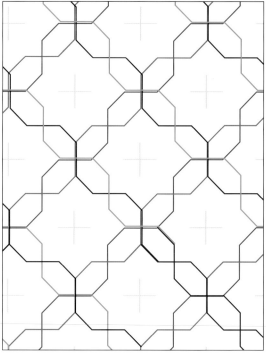

DESIGN 5:8
Bishamon
BISHAMON

毘沙門

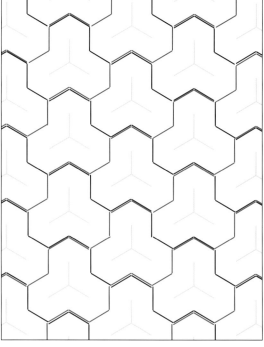

126

DESIGN 5:9
Arare Kikko
HAILSTONE

霰亀甲

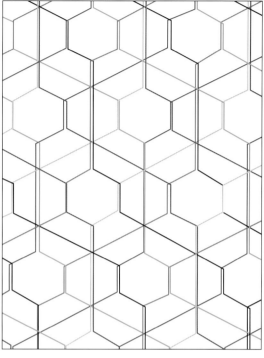

DESIGN 5:10
Mukai-Kikko
FACED TORTOISESHELL

向い亀甲

copies of the design engraved on the armored breastplate that Bishamon was depicted as wearing. Use of this design in sashiko conveyed a wish for increased wealth.

HAILSTONE

The *arare kikko* (hailstone) pattern shown in design 5:9 uses exactly the same shape as the *bishamon* design shown on the preceding page, but arrays those shapes such that a hexagon is formed in between them. The three-pronged design that was sewn in the middle of the *bishamon* design has also been considerably elongated. These lines in turn form larger laterally stretched out hexagons. The design came to be associated with hail (*arare*). The use of the *bishamon* shape in a pattern labeled as *kikko* makes it clear that *bishamon* patterns are themselves variants of *kikko*. The god Bishamon probably is shown wearing *kikko* patterned armor as both a charm for and a boast of longevity.

FACED TORTOISESHELL

The *mukai-kikko* (faced tortoiseshell) pattern abstracts the tortoiseshell shape to an even greater degree. Design 5:10 is widely used in modern Japan for pieced quilts as well as for sashiko stitching. This design also shows that frequently only segments of the hexagonal *kikko* design were used in sashiko stitching patterns.

-ARROW FEATHERS

The version of *yabane* (arrow feathers) shown in design 5:1 is perhaps the most popular in modern Japan. I stitched the mirror-imaged rows in red to emphasize how closely this pattern's design line is related to the line that forms the *hirayama-michi* (design 3:2). The *yabane* line is stitched on the diagonal rather than the horizontal axis, and it pivots with 60- and 120-degree angles rather than right angles, but the basic movement of the two lines is identical. This design is as easy to stitch as the *hirayama-michi* if your stitch length is calibrated correctly.

CYPRESS FENCE

Design 5:12 gives the version of *higaki* (cypress fence) that is best suited to continuous stitching. Another version uses a right-angle pivot and, consequently, produces a greater overlap on the "v" shape used in continuous stitching. The right angle version is therefore much less attractive when double stitched. The *higaki* pattern represents the design made by the weaving of cypress slats into a fence. It is interesting to compare this design with the sashiko pattern representative of another woven pattern, *kagome* (designs 1:11 through 1:13).

DESIGN 5:11
Yabane
ARROW FEATHERS

矢羽

DESIGN 5:12
Higaki
CYPRESS FENCE

葉垣

DESIGN 5:13
Ishiguruma
STONE WHEEL

石車

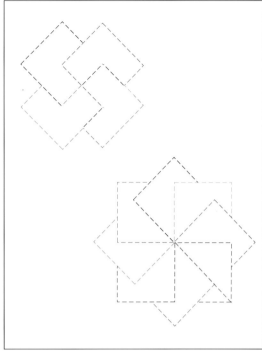

DESIGN 5:14
Hiragumi Manji
SUN MOTIF

平組まん字

STONE WHEEL

The two patterns shown in design 5:13 are both called *ishiguruma* (stone wheel). The lines intersecting in the center of the first *ishiguruma* design show the classic *manji* (Buddhist cross) shape. This design is also the building block of the pattern called *hiragumi manji*, shown in design 5:14. The second *ishiguruma* design involves a simple rotation and overlay of the original design such that eight intersecting lines are formed. In the Nara and Heian periods, only high-ranking courtiers could wear clothing embellished with designs like these that were based on the *koshi* grid. Checked patterns were strictly forbidden to lower-ranking courtiers and the common people. By the Edo period, however, this restriction on the use of *koshi* patterns was eased. Various design books even recommended the second version of the design as a classic representation of the stone wheel of carts used in Japan to transport goods.

HIRAGUMI MANJI

The *manji* design shown in design 5:14 is often used in modern sashiko. The dotted line indicates an extension that is sewn by pivoting out from the solid line, stitching to the end of the dotted line, and then returning in the same needle holes.

The *hirasan-kuzushi* pattern shown in design 5:15 is a variant of the *ishidatami* (paving stone) pattern in which three rectangular paving stones are placed alternately along the vertical and horizontal axes in such a way that a square in formed at the intersection of each four sets. The *hirasan-kuzushi* (simplified paving block) pattern was developed in modern sashiko as a simpler way to obtain the look of the *ishidatami* pattern. In it, the sets of three paving stones are laid directly against one another as they are rotated vertically and horizontally. No complicating interior square is formed. Sew each of the interior lines twice. Pivot on to the interior lines when they intersect with the long continuous lines that frame the design. Next stitch each internal intersecting line by pivoting onto it and then turning the fabric around and stitching back in the same needle holes to the starting point.

DIAMOND-SHAPED WAVES

Design 5:16 is the *hishi-seigaiha* (diamond-shaped waves) pattern. It is stitched in the same manner as the *hirasan-kuzushi.* Pivot onto the interior angled lines as they intersect with the long continuous lines. Stitch each interior angled line to the end, turn the fabric around and stitch back, continuing on the long framing line until the next intersection point.

DESIGN 5:15
Hirasan-Kuzushi
SIMPLIFIED PAVING BLOCKS

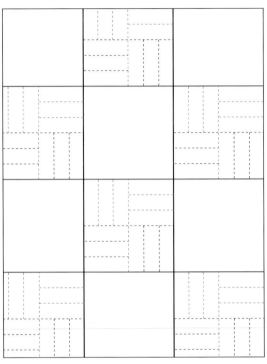

DESIGN 5:16
Hishi Seigaiha
DIAMOND-SHAPED WAVES

菱青海波

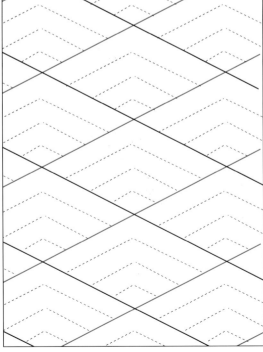

DESIGN 6:1
Matsunami
WAVES OF PINE

松波

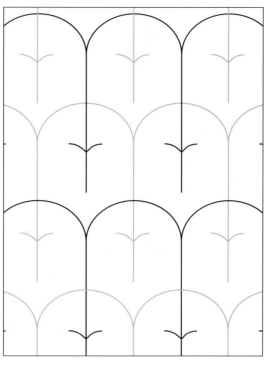

DESIGN 6:2
Ume No Hana
PLUM BLOSSOM AND JANOME
JAPANESE SNAKE'S EYE, BULL'S EYE, OR TWISTED DOUBLE-RING

梅の花
蛇の目

WAVES OF PINE

The *matsunami* (waves of pine) pattern shown in design 6:1 dates back at least to 1824. At the beginning of their calendar year in midwinter, the Japanese adorn their gates or their door frames with pine boughs. The long vertical lines and the small curved extensions are double stitched. Stitch the long vertical line completely, turn the fabric around (leaving the needle down in the fabric), and stitch back to the junction with the small curved extensions, then pivot onto the line of the curve, stitch it, turn the fabric around, and stitch back to the vertical line. Repeat for the other side.

PLUM BLOSSOM, SNAKE'S EYE, BULL'S EYE, OR TWISTED DOUBLE-RING

The two patterns in design 6:2 show how one basic shape can signify very different things. An unadorned, five-circle shape always represents *ume no hana* (plum blossom) even if no additional curved lines are added in the center to represent stamens. The plum blossom has deep significance for the Japanese: it braves the winter cold to produce flowers, serves as the harbinger of spring, and represents courage. The plum motif was particularly popular in the Nara and Heian periods. The same five-circle shape becomes the *janome*, or snake's eye, motif when small interior circles are added.

CRANE (ORIGINAL DESIGN)

Japanese crest designs of the *tsuru* (crane) often take the top half of a flower pattern and add a bird's neck below as in design 6:3. The design is sewn with only two curved and pivoting lines. The arc that serves as the demarcation between the crane's body and wings is double stitched, as are the lines between the wings and tail feathers. The *tsuru* design was one of several associated with longevity in many Oriental cultures. In Japan, *tsuru* was sometimes used to decorate the backs of hand mirrors as a charm against wrinkles and other unwanted signs of aging.

CHERRY BLOSSOMS (ORIGINAL DESIGN)

The *sakura* (cherry blossom) design is always shown with five notched petals. This feature helps distinguish highly stylized cherry blossoms from other flowers. *Sakura* is a symbol of spring. Cherry trees grew wild around Nara and Kyoto. In Heian times, the cherry blossom began to be considered the Japanese national flower. Cherry blossom viewing ceremonies began, and the cherry blossom was often simply referred to as *hana*, the Japanese word for flower. The transference of admiration from plum blossoms to cherry blossoms appears to mark the beginning of the development of an independent Japanese aesthetic. My design 6:4 is stitched very much like the *nashi* pattern (design 4:10).

DESIGN 6:3
Tsuru
CRANE (ORIGINAL DESIGN)

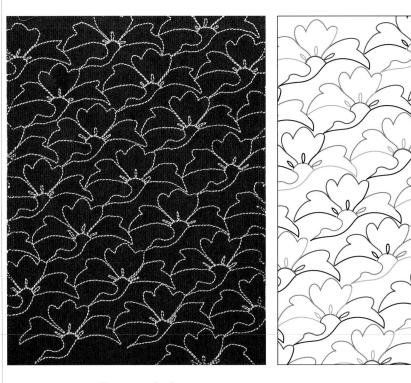

DESIGN 6:4
Sakura
CHERRY BLOSSOMS (ORIGINAL DESIGN)

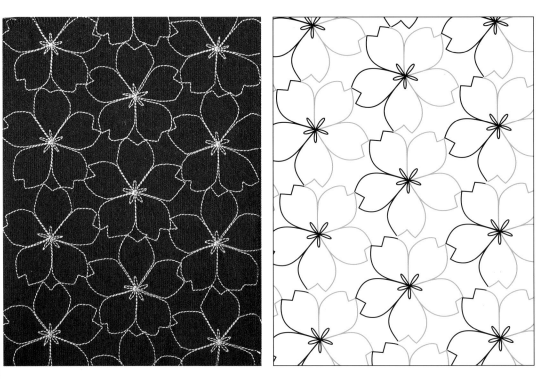

DESIGN 6:5
Fuji
WISTERIA (ORIGINAL DESIGN)

藤

DESIGN 6:6
Take
BAMBOO (ORIGINAL DESIGN)

竹

WISTERIA (ORIGINAL DESIGN)

The Japanese transplanted wisteria to formal gardens and trained it to grow on structures that let the blossoms show to full advantage. During the middle of the Heian period, courtiers held wisteria viewing parties when the plant was in bloom. As the Fujiwara family rose in prominence during the late Heian period, the visual presence of wisteria also increased. Design 6:5 is stitched with six identical curved lines. The straight lines through the center are double stitched. They can be sewn on any one of the passes that the six curved lines make through the center of the design.

BAMBOO (ORIGINAL DESIGN)

Although take (bamboo) was imported from China, it became an essential building material for the rural Japanese. Bamboo leaves were also used to wrap food, and numerous household items were crafted from bamboo stalks. Because it stayed green during the winter and rarely broke, even when under a heavy weight of snow, it came to symbolize resilience and perseverance. Take, ume no hana (plum blossom), and matsu (pine) are called "three companions of deep cold" by the Japanese and are often represented together in arts and crafts. Particularly when used in association with the other two motifs, bamboo came to represent some of the highest ideals of Japanese society: integrity, steadfastness, honor, and purity.

In design 6:6, the diagonal koshi grid and the nami-like large arcs are stitched only once. The rest of the design is double stitched from the node where the koshi grid intersects the zenith of the nami arc.

CHRYSANTHEMUM

The *kiku* (chrysanthemum) symbolizes autumn. The 16-petal chrysanthemum was once reserved for the emperor's use. A chrysanthemum viewing festival is held each year. One of its traditional activities is on the night before, to spread a loosely woven fabric like cheesecloth on chrysanthemum blooms in the garden, and to gather it later heavy with dew. Washing one's face with this was believed to enhance life expectancy and appearance. Chrysanthemum petals were also floated on the plum wine, *sake*. Several different variations on *kiku* are shown in quarter section in design 6:7. The chrysanthemum motif was most often stitched in that manner so that the threads could be gathered at the corner and knotted together to form a tassel.

FOLDING FANS

In addition to developing *kiku* designs that resembled fans, sashiko also used fans as a motif. *Senmen* fan designs are distinguished from *kiku* designs by their outer edge. *(Kiku's* edges are ruffled while senmen's edges are one smooth circle.)* Folding fans were a Japanese innovation and were a chief export to China. Persons of rank always carried a fan to symbolize authority and power. To stitch design 6:8, begin on one of the long, pivoting curved lines, stopping to double stitch the lines radiating out from the center point of each fan as it is reached. Complete the other parts of the design in this same manner.

DESIGN 6:7
Kiku
CHRYSANTHEMUM

DESIGN 6:8
Senmen
FOLDING FANS

扇面

DESIGN 6:9

Tachibana
MANDARIN ORANGE BLOSSOM (ORIGINAL DESIGN)

Kakitsubata
IRIS (ORIGINAL DESIGN)

橘
燕子花

DESIGN 6:10

Choji and Matsu
PINE (ORIGINAL DESIGN)

丁字
松

MANDARIN ORANGE BLOSSOM

The *tachibana* (Mandarin orange blossom) was imported to Japan from China during the Tumulus period. In modern Japan, families who have one or more daughters in the household display orange blossoms along with their doll collections during the annual Girl's Festival. My original pattern shown in design 6:9 can be sewn as a single or double border.

IRIS

The kakitsubata (iris) came into particular prominence during the Heian period. Iris viewing festivals were inaugurated then, a tradition that continues today. Both of my original patterns shown in design 6:9 can be sewn either as a single or double border.

CLOVE

The *choji* (clove) was first imported into Japan during the Heian period and came to epitomize luxury. The pattern shown in design 6:10 is very close to the traditional depiction of the clove in Japanese crests. To embroider it on a garment is to wish the recipient the "best of everything."

PINE

Those who are not familiar with Japanese motifs often misinterpret *matsu* (pine tree) patterns as representing clouds. Most *matsu* patterns have the general shape shown in the lower part of design 6:10. Detail such as the roots and the pinecones may be omitted or elaborated upon. In all these patterns, dotted lines indicate double stitching.

ARROW FEATHERS

An abstract *yabane* (arrow feathers) is shown in design 7:1. Although threads have to be knotted and tied, double stitching makes this design approachable for a machine sewer because the number of knots is cut in half and the threads are less likely to pull out. The *yoko-jima* stripe shown in design 1:4 gives this *yabane* design its basic structure, but periodic interrupting of stitching has created a very different overall design.

CRISSCROSS VARIATION

Interrupted line segments also form a design that resembles a tic-tac-toe grid. The first pattern in design 7:2 is called *hirai-jumon* (crisscross). By double stitching each line, and pivoting periodically at a junction with a new line, the entire *hirai-jumon* design can be stitched continuously before returning to the starting point. Only one knot is required.

LATTICED IKAT

When the single line from the *hirai-jumon* pattern is doubled, another design, known as *koshi-gasuri* (latticed ikat), is formed. Ikat is an age-old textile design technique in which skeins of yarn are tied at pre-determined points before being dyed to prevent the penetration of dye which creates patterns when the yarn is woven. One of these patterns closely resembles this sashiko design. The *koshi-gasuri* pattern shown on the lower portion of design 7:2 is associated with summer.

DESIGN 7:1
Yabane
ARROW FEATHERS

矢羽

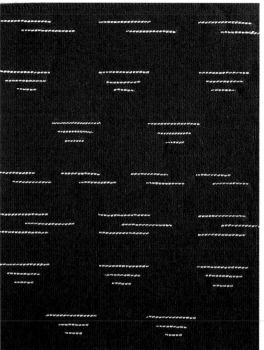

DESIGN 7:2
Hirai-Jumon CRISSCROSS VARIATION
Koshi-Gasuri LATTICED IKAT

平井十文
格子絣

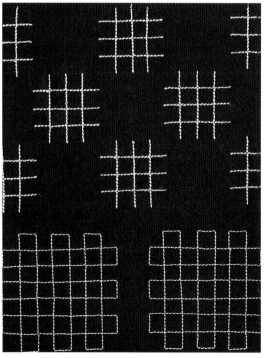

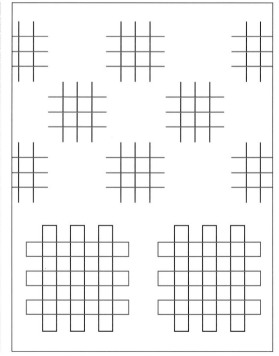

DESIGN 7:3
Masu-Sashi
MEASURING BOXES

桝刺し

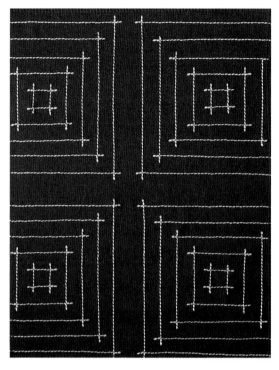

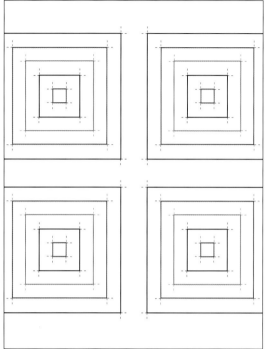

DESIGN 7:4
Tsumeta
RICE FIELDS

積め田

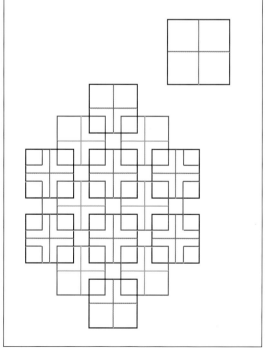

The *masu-sashi* (measuring boxes) pattern is used two ways. Several patterns may be stitched so that they form a larger pattern, as is shown in design 7:3, or a single pattern with many, many component boxes that gradually increase in size may be used. *(Masu* is the Japanese word for "increase.") The design may simply represent the set of "nesting" boxes found in almost every Japanese home in ancient times. The smallest box was used to drink *sake*, and the larger boxes were used to measure out ingredients for cooking, such as rice. The boxes are also said to be a symbolic representation of the value of the labor that various members contributed to the household. The labor of children and women was less valuable, as shown by the smaller boxes, while the labor of men was more valuable, as shown by the larger boxes. In any event, over time, the size of the box also came to be associated with the age of the wearer. The oldest residents of the household wore clothing stitched with the most and the largest boxes. When stitching the pattern, pivot to stitch the extensions at each corner as in *igeta ni hakkuku* (design 5:6) so that each box can be sewn continuously.

RICE FIELDS

The *tsumeta* (rice fields) sashiko pattern is one of several taken directly from *kanji*. It is an almost exact representation of the ideograph meaning rice fields. The design can be stitched in one continuous motion if you begin at the top of the cross and double stitch all its lines then stitch the square frame. Overlaying *tsumeta* patterns on top of each other as shown on design 7:4 creates an extremely attractive pattern. By pivoting when another square intersects the line you are sewing, you can sew the entire outline of the tsumeta squares in one continuous motion. The internal crosses can then be stitched later.

CHECK PATTERN USING THE LETTER "I"

Like the *tsumeta* pattern, the *koshi-kuzushi* pattern comes from the written Japanese language. The letter "I" comes first in the Japanese alphabet. It has associations for the Japanese as the letter "A" does for Westerners. Double stitching each line of the "I" allows each one in design 7:5 to be sewn with only one knot. It also secures stitching that might otherwise pull out easily. The stitching can begin anywhere on the "I" since you will end up wherever you started.

FOUR-DIAMOND PATTERN

OVERLAPPING DIAMONDS

Independently sewn *hishi* shapes were also frequently used in sashiko. The two patterns shown in design 7:6, *yotsugumi hishi* (four-diamond pattern) and *narihira waribishi* (overlapping diamond), can both be sewn continuously if you pivot from one diamond to another.

DESIGN 7:5
Koshi-Kuzushi
CHECK PATTERN USING THE LETTER "I"

格子崩し

DESIGN 7:6
Yotsugumi Hishi FOUR-DIAMOND PATTERN
Narihira Waribishi OVERLAPPING DIAMONDS

四つ組菱
形平割菱

138

DESIGN 7:7
Kikko
TORTOISE SHELLS

亀甲

DESIGN 7:8
Seigaiha
BLUE OCEAN WAVES

青海波

TORTOISE SHELLS

One of the most common *kikko* (tortoiseshell) patterns is shown in design 7:7. Although it cannot be sewn completely with a continuous stitch, much of the pattern can, as shown by the color coding.

BLUE OCEAN WAVES

Although the seigaiha version of the wave design dates back to ancient Persia, it became associated with Buddhism as it migrated eastward over the centuries. The design entered Japanese culture at the same time that Buddhism did in the Asuka period. However, neither the Nami or Seigaiha form of the wave motif became popular until the Heian period. During the Heian period, the name *seigaiha* was even given to one of the dances performed in a scene described in the world's first novel, *The Tale of the Genji*, which was written by Lady Murasaki Shikibu

The *seigaiha* pattern shown in design 7:8 is also one of the most common designs and is stitched in much the same manner as the *hishi-seigaiha* pattern shown in design 5:16. However, because calibrating stitch length for differing sizes of arcs is more complicated than calibrating the stitch length for differing lengths of straight lines, sewers may be less frustrated if they sew the interior arcs separately after they have sewn the frame of the design. Each arc should be double stitched, both to cut down on the number of knots and to secure the stitching.

FOUR-RING PATTERN

THREE-RING PATTERN

Although the *yotsuwa-chigai* (four ring) pattern and the *mitsuwa* (three ring) patterns shown in design 8:1 may look Celtic to Westerners, they are both thoroughly Japanese. The *yotsuwa-chi-gai* was used on family crests to represent interlocking, forged-iron rings. The *mitsuwa* was even more widely used as a crest motif, but apparently was meant only as an abstract design of interwoven circles, perhaps recalling the *shippo* pattern. Both would be well suited as a focal design in a large project such as a quilt.

INTERLOCKING
TORTOISESHELLS

TRIPLE TORTOISESHELLS

Many hexagon-based sashiko patterns were also derived from crest designs, among them various *bishamon* patterns (see design 5:8) and *mukai-kikko* (design 5:10) as well as the *musubi-kuzushi* (interlocking tortoise-shells) motif and the *mitsugumi-kikko* (triple tortoise-shells) patterns shown in design 8:2. Although they require some knot tying, their beauty justifies the time spent sewing them.

DESIGN 8:1
Yotsuwa-Chigai Mitsuwa
FOUR-RING PATTERN
THREE-RING PATTERN

四つ輪血会
三輪

DESIGN 8:2
Musubi-Kuzushi Mitsugumi-Kikko
INTERLOCKING TORTOISESHELLS
TRIPLE TORTOISESHELLS

結び崩し
三組亀甲

DESIGN 8:3
Kikyo
BALLOONFLOWER

桔梗

DESIGN 8:4
Sakura
CHERRY BLOSSOM

桜

BALLOONFLOWER

The Japanese often completely abstracted the essential defining features of a pattern, as is illustrated by the two crests shown in design 8:3 and 8:4. Despite their high degree of geometrical abstraction, both are still identifiable to someone familiar with the conventions by which these flowers were drawn. Although they both have five petals, it is unlikely someone would confuse the two.

The petals of the *kikyo* end in an outward point. The *kikyo* is known as the "balloonflower" or "bellflower" to western gardeners. It is a symbol of autumn and, in the Nara period, was established as one of the seven plants of autumn. (The other six were bush clover, pampas grass, arrowroot, pinks, valerian, and eupatorium.) The *kikyo* was a popular crest of the warrior class during Japan's feudal period.

CHERRY BLOSSOM

In contrast, the petals of the *sakura* (cherry blossom) are indented and show the characteristic "notch." This allows them to be rendered as heart-shapes in the crest pattern. The *sakura* is a symbol of spring. It was used much less frequently as a crest design.

The Japanese admired the *hoya* (mistletoe) particularly because of its symmetrical growth pattern. Design 8:5 is typical of *hoya* crest patterns. Like the *tomoe* design, the *hoya* motif was associated with the god of war, Hachiman, and, for that reason, it was a popular crest with the warrior class.

CARRIAGE WHEEL

The *genji-guruma*, shown in design 8:6, is a more elaborate version of the *ishi-guruma* (cartwheel) motif (design 5:13).

DESIGN 8:5
Hoya
MISTLETOE

ホヤ

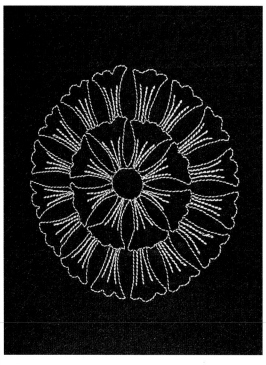

DESIGN 8:6
Genji-guruma
CARRIAGE WHEEL

源氏車

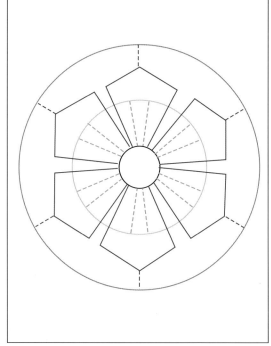

桔梗

桜

BALLOONFLOWER

The Japanese often completely abstracted the essential defining features of a pattern, as is illustrated by the two crests shown in design 8:3 and 8:4. Despite their high degree of geometrical abstraction, both are still identifiable to someone familiar with the conventions by which these flowers were drawn. Although they both have five petals, it is unlikely someone would confuse the two.

The petals of the *kikyo* end in an outward point. The *kikyo* is known as the "balloonflower" or "bellflower" to western gardeners. It is a symbol of autumn and, in the Nara period, was established as one of the seven plants of autumn. (The other six were bush clover, pampas grass, arrowroot, pinks, valerian, and eupatorium.) The *kikyo* was a popular crest of the warrior class during Japan's feudal period.

CHERRY BLOSSOM

In contrast, the petals of the *sakura* (cherry blossom) are indented and show the characteristic "notch." This allows them to be rendered as heart-shapes in the crest pattern. The *sakura* is a symbol of spring. It was used much less frequently as a crest design.

MISTLETOE

The Japanese admired the *hoya* (mistletoe) particularly because of its symmetrical growth pattern. Design 8:5 is typical of *hoya* crest patterns. Like the *tomoe* design, the *hoya* motif was associated with the god of war, Hachiman, and, for that reason, it was a popular crest with the warrior class.

ホヤ

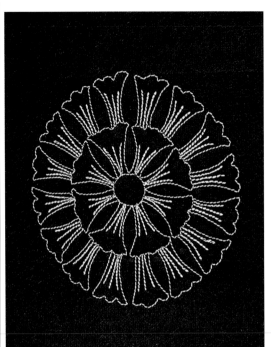

源氏車

CARRIAGE WHEEL

The *genji-guruma*, shown in design 8:6, is a more elaborate version of the *ishi-guruma* (cartwheel) motif (design 5:13).

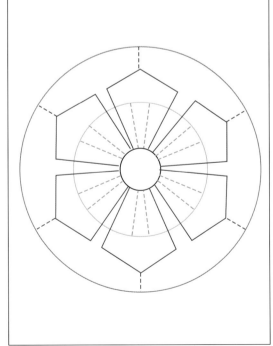

BIBLIOGRAPHY

SASHIKO DESIGN AND HISTORY

Allen, Alice. *Sashiko Made Simple: Japanese Quilting by Machine.* Hinsdale: Bernina Books of America, 1992.

Classic Quilting of Sashiko, The. Tokyo: Ondorisha Publishers Ltd., 1990.

Matsunaga, Karen Kim. *Japanese County Quilting: Sashiko Patterns and Projects for Beginners.* Tokyo: Kodansha International, 1990.

Mende, Kazuko and Reiko Morishige. *Sashiko: Blue and White Quilt Art of Japan.* Tokyo: Shufunotomo/Japan Publications, 1991.

Ogikubo, Kiyoko. *Kogin and Sashiko Stitch. Volume 13 of Kyoto Shoin's Art Library of Japanese Textiles.* Kyoto: Fujioka Mamoru Kyoto Shoin Co. Ltd., 1993.

Ota, Kim. *Sashiko Quilting.* Seattle, 1981.

Rostocki, Janet K. *Twelve Treasures Advanced Sashiko for Machine Sewing: Contemporary Japanese Style Quilting.* Vandalia: Summa Design, 1998.

Rostocki, Janet K. *Sashiko for Machine Sewing: Japanese-Style Quilting Classic to Contemporary.* Dayton: Summa Design, 1988.

Sanders, Jan. *A.B.C's of Machine Sashiko.* Michigan City: Communications Concepts, 1995.

Sashiko: Traditional Japanese Quilt Designs. Tokyo: Nihon Vogue Publishing Co. Ltd., 1989.

Takano, Saikoh. *Sashiko and Beyond: Techniques and Projects for Quilting in the Japanese Style.* Radnor: Chilton Book Company, 1993.

Yoshida, Eiko. *Sashiko.* Toyko: Ondorisha, 1993.

JAPANESE TEXTILES AND TRADITIONAL JAPANESE DESIGNS WORKED IN MEDIA OTHER THAN SASHIKO

Liddell, Jill and Yuko Watanabe. *Japanese Quilts*. New York: E. P. Dutton, 1988.

Marshall, John. *Make Your Own Japanese Clothes: Patterns and Idea for Modern Wear.* Tokyo: Kodansha International, 1988.

Sudo, Kumiko. *Circles of the East.* Lincolnwood: The Quilt Digest Press, 1997.

Sudo, Kumiko. *East Quilts West.* Lincolnwood: The Quilt Digest Press, 1992.

Tamura, Shiji. *The Techniques of Japanese Embroidery.* The Japanese Embroidery Center. Iola: Krause Publications, 1998.

Yoshimoto, Kaman. *Textile Design I: Traditional Japanese Small Motif.* Singapore: Page One Publishing Pte Limited, 1993.

Yoshimoto, Kaman. *Textile Design I: Arabesque.* Singapore: Page One Publishing Pte Limited, 1993.

Yoshimoto, Kaman. *Textile Design III: Traditional Stripes and Latices.* Singapore: Page One Publishing Pte Limited, 1993.

Yoshimoto, Kaman. *Textile Design IIV: Traditional Sarasatic.* Singapore: Page One Publishing Pte Limited, 1994.

JAPANESE DESIGN, GENERAL

Adachi, Fumie, trans. *Japanese Design Motifs: 4,260 Illustrations of Japanese Crests Compiled by the Matsuya Piece-Goods Store.* New York: Dover Publications Inc., 1972.

Allen, Jeannie. *Designer's Guide to Japanese Patterns 2.* San Francisco: Chronicle Books, 1988. (Based on Edo Mon-yo Jiten by Katano Takashi.)

Allen, Jeannie. *Designer's Guide to Japanese Patterns 3.* San Francisco: Chronicle Books, 1989. (Based on Oh-cho Mon-yo Jiten by Katano Takashi.)

Amstutz, Walter, ed. *Japanese Emblems and Designs.* New York: Dover Publications Inc., 1970.

D'Addetta, Joseph. *Traditional Japanese Design Motifs with 264 Illustrations.* New York: Dover Publications Inc., 1984.

Dover, John W. *The Elements of Japanese Design: A Handbook or Family Crests, Heraldry & Symbolism.* New York: Weatherhill Inc., 1971.

Grafton, Carol Belanger. *Treasury of Japanese Designs and Motifs for Artists and Craftsmen.* Mineola, NY: Dover Publications Inc., 1983.

Hillier, J. *Japanese Color Prints.* London: Phaidon Press Limited, 1991.

Hornung, Clarence, ed. *Traditional Japanese Crest Designs.* Mineola, NY: Dover Publications Inc., 1985.

Hornung, Clarence, ed. *Traditional Japanese Stencil Designs.* Mineola, NY: Dover Publications Inc, 1985.

Japanese Border Designs Selected and Edited by Theodore Menten with 463 Illustrations. New York: Dover Publications Inc, 1975. This is a selection of illustrations from the Japanese Book Kodai Moshiki Zuko (Picture Album of Traditional Patterns, no place, no date.)

Orban-Szontagh, Madeleine. *Japanese Floral Patterns and Motifs.* New York: Dover Publications, Inc., 1990. General Background and Japanese Language and Culture

Furse, Raymond. *Japan: An Invitation.* Rutland: Charles E. Tuttle Company, 1991.

Henshall, Kenneth G. *A Guide to Remembering Kanji Characters.* Rutland: Tuttle Language Library, Charles E. Tuttle Company, 1988.

Kindaichi, Haruhiko. *The Japanese Language.* trans. Umeyo Hirano. Rutland: Tuttle Language Library, Charles E. Tuttle Company, 1978.

Miura, Akira. *Japanese Words and Their Uses.* Rutland: Charles E. Tuttle Company, 1983.

Yanagi, Soetsu. *The Unknown Craftsman: A Japanese Insight Into Beauty.* Tokyo: Kodansha International, 1972 and 1989.

ACKNOWLEDGEMENTS

So many people contributed to this book, either directly or indirectly that it is impossible to thank them all for their inspiration, encouragement, and suggestions. However, my most important supporter cannot be neglected: my husband, John Rukavina, who endured with such incredibly good grace many months of my not really listening to what he said because I was thinking about THE BOOK (and who also contributed in so many other ways to the book's success). Special thanks also to those who have hosted my sashiko classes over the years: Sally Hickerson, owner of Waechter's Silk Shop in Asheville, NC; Rosemary Hargrove, owner of The Cotton Boll in Chapel Hill, NC; Nancy Meridith, owner of Sew 'n Seams in Greensboro, NC; and Marilyn Harlow, owner of Bernina World of Sewing in Raleigh, NC. I wish it were also possible to list all the students from whom I've learned so much. I would be remiss not to thank Anne Davidson and Pat Thomas, both of Chapel Hill, NC, for loaning their clothing to be photographed. Other students who made their own special contributions are Helen Blocker of Johnson City, TN; Shirley Sharpe of Asheville, NC; Jeannette Paulson of Greensboro NC; and Louise Malefyt of Carrboro, NC. And special thanks to the staff at Lark Books who did truly made this project a "Lark."

The editor and art director would like to thank The Larson family of Leister, NC, Stephanie Clark of Asheville, NC, and Sandy Stambaugh of Asheville, NC, for generously lending their homes to us for photography. They would also like to thank Nicole Tuggle for modeling the sashiko garments with such beauty and grace.